/981

St. Benedict,

Blessed by God

Guy-Marie Oury, O.S.B.

Translated by
Rev. John A. Otto

the liturgical press
Collegeville   Minnesota

Library of Congress Cataloging in Publication Data

Oury, Guy Marie.
    St. Benedict, blessed by God.

    Translation of Ce que croyait Benoît.
    Bibliography: p.
    1. Benedictus, Saint, Abbot of Monte Cassino.
I.   Title.
BX4700.B30913   271'.1'024   80-13253
ISBN 0-8146-1181-8

Nihil obstat: Joseph C. Kremer, S.T.L., *Censor deputatus. Imprimatur:*
✝ George H. Speltz, Bishop of St. Cloud, St. Cloud, Minnesota, March 6,
1980.

    This book is a translation of *Ce que croyait Benoît*, Les Nouvelles Edi-
tions MAME, Paris, 1974.

Contents

Introduction

The followers of the monastic tradition of St. Benedict have reason to rejoice during the fifteenth centenary of his birth. The monastic movement is still a characteristic feature of the Church of Christ and the *Rule of Benedict* is still a directive force of this movement. The Rule still provides the basic directions of the monastic life today: it teaches a program of communal and private prayer; it advocates a schedule of reflective reading that leads to a prayerful attention to God; it promotes a leadership of service and wisdom; it demands a community of goods; it requires a mode of hospitality; and it outlines a method of fraternal existence.

These and other features of the *Rule of Benedict* provide direction for monastic life today, though it is true that they are transformed and expressed differently. The monastic movement as an inspiration of the Holy Spirit within the Christian Church draws heavily upon the manner in which Benedict assimilated the features of monasticism in existence before his time. But since the movement lives continually under the power of the Spirit, it shapes the features of the monastery to the modes and manners of the twentieth century. The movement is alive, and it is alive precisely because it continues to unfold from one age to the next, from one culture to the next. And the *Rule of Benedict* is still an inspiration for monasticism today because it unites within itself the concern for community and the need for a solitary pursuit of God in prayer. It is still an inspiration for monasticism today because it brings to focus essential features of the life of the Church: search for God, public worship, private prayer, charismatic leadership, community life, mutual service, hospitality, stewardship of goods. These dimensions of the Church become the foci of the monastic life.

This book will serve as another tribute to Benedict of Nursia, to the *Rule of Benedict*, and to the long tradition of Benedictine monasticism. It is not written solely for monastic readers though they will run through the pages with profit, being reminded of the basic reasons why they made monastic profession. It is written for all religious who see dimensions of the monastic movement at the origin of their own mode of life and profession. It is written for any Christian who wishes to discover traditional and proved norms for seeking God, of prayer, of assembling in Christ, and of loving God.

St. Benedict, Blessed by God highlights features of the *Rule of Benedict* and makes them available for quiet reflection today. It is a book that is in contact with current scholarship on the origin and meaning of the Rule while it avoids detailed documentation of sources. It permits an easy access to the spiritual treasures of the Rule and to a sane reflection on the effectiveness of the Rule for monastic life today. In fact, the reflections are there for any Christian to assimilate. Formal profession in the monastic life is not required for a fruitful pursuit of the word and the love of God, the practice of prayerful attention to God, the following of Christ in hope and community. The author, himself a monk, offers the very best of the *Rule of Benedict* for the enrichment of the monastic profession today and for the Christian life anywhere.

March 21, 1980

Jerome Theisen, O.S.B.
Abbot of St. John's Abbey
Collegeville, Minnesota

St. Benedict, Blessed by God

1

the Life and Rule of St. Benedict

When Constantius was bishop of Albi (ca. 627), Venerandus, a nobleman of his diocese, sent him a manuscript containing "the Rule of St. Benedict, Roman abbot," with the request that it be kept in the archives of his cathedral church. The bishop was also to see that the Rule was observed by the abbot and monks of the small monastery of Altaripa, a stipulation that was part of an agreement some years earlier between Venerandus, the founder, and Bishop St. Fibicius, uncle of Constantius.

Venerandus provides the first certain mention of the spread of St. Benedict's Rule beyond the confines of its origin. In the year 593 or 594, Pope St. Gregory the Great had noted its existence in his Dialogues: "He [Benedict] wrote a Rule for monks that is remarkable for its discretion and its clarity of language. Anyone who wishes to know more about his life and character can discover in his Rule exactly what he was like as abbot, for his life could not have differed from his teaching" (D 36).[1]

---

[1] Book II of the *Dialogues of St. Gregory* (which deals with St. Benedict) is cited from *Life and Miracles of St. Benedict*, trans. Odo J. Zimmermann, O.S.B., and Benedict R. Avery, O.S.B. (Collegeville, Minnesota: The Liturgical Press, 1949).
The letter D and the number stand for Book II of the Dialogues and the section.

It is highly probable that this pontifical recommendation helped to make the Rule known and to assure its success. At the time of St. Benedict's death, most likely between 540–550, his Rule was followed only in some monasteries of central Italy. By the ninth century it had supplanted, in the Carolingian Empire, virtually all other Rules — some thirty in number — that were being used by monks of the Latin West. In the twelfth century it held sway, unrivaled, from Scandinavia to Sicily, from Ireland to Poland, from Spain to Palestine. It was even practiced by a convent of nuns buried in the snows of Eystribygd, Greenland. The history of Benedictine monachism is the history of this Rule fashioning, little by little, the entire far-flung complex of Latin monastic communities.

For this reason it can be said that Benedictines, unlike other religious families, do not really have a founder; or rather, they have a multitude of founders. To Benedictines, St. Benedict is not so much founder as lawgiver, master, and teacher of spiritual doctrine. It is in this capacity that he is father and founder to them. Instead of representing, as do other Rules, a stage in the evolution of monachism, Benedict's Rule in its most essential parts became the permanent and definitive norm of the monastic life pursued in common. But thanks to the Rule's remarkable flexibility, monachism was not frozen into one invariable type. The Rule adapted itself to places, to times, to civilizations, to the spiritual aspirations of generations of disciples among whom it nevertheless maintained the strong Benedictine bond of kinship.

What, for example, could be more dissimilar on the human plane than a Monte Cassino monk of the sixth century and a Maurist of the seventeenth; than a member of the great Carolingian communities and an African monk today; than a follower of the "new" monasticism of the twelfth century and a son of Dom Guéranger? Yet in the various realizations of the Benedictine monastic ideal there are many points of contact, many basic similarities. The spiritual configuration of the disciple of St. Benedict remains essentially the same in all forms of Benedictinism because the same Rule inspired and left its mark on them.

The man whose work would become the common patrimony of Western monks was born at Nursia in the Sabine hills, toward the end of the fifth century (ca. 480). He was sent to Rome for his early education but when still very young embarked upon the ascetical life as the way that would lead him safely to God. He practiced this life at Affile (Enfide). His next step, prompted by a desire for greater solitude, was to settle in a grotto at Subiaco, where he spent some years as a hermit. The monks of Vicovaro then made him their abbot, but this first venture ended in frustration, and Benedict returned to Subiaco. His life again attracted disciples who gathered around him. Eventually, accompanied by some monks he settled at the top of Monte Cassino and became the spiritual father of several communities of monks for whom he wrote his Rule. Latin monasticism was already two hundred years old. (St. Martin had founded it about the year 361 with a monastery in Gaul, at Ligugé.)

*

What is the basic material available for treating of the mind and message of St. Benedict? Where can one go to find what he believed? To what extent does his written work reveal the man? And who are the witnesses who can tell us what it was that gave his spiritual life its particular orientation?

Benedict of Nursia left us his "Rule for monasteries": a prologue and seventy-three chapters. The work is not voluminous, only some hundred pages in pocket size. Nevertheless, compared with other Rules of that time, some of which were no more than a few pages, it is one of the most complete and most extensive monastic codes we have.

Less than fifty years after Benedict's death Pope Gregory the Great wrote a sort of biography in the form of a dialogue. The Pope based his work on the testimony of four of Benedict's monks who had lived under Benedict: Constantine, his successor at Monte Cassino; Valentinian, abbot of the monastery at the Lateran; Simplicius, third abbot of Cassino; and Honoratus, abbot of Subiaco. The latter was still living when Gregory wrote the Dialogues and probably had been a disciple only indirectly.

Book II of the Dialogues

The recourse to firsthand witnesses is impressive. But the Pope did not approach his task in the manner of a modern historian, sifting his data for accuracy. His aim was to provide spiritual instruction and to illustrate it from the life of various saintly persons, mostly from central Italy. The Dialogues were destined to be a great success, a "best seller." Pope Zachary (741–752) translated them into Greek; they were also translated into Arabic and Anglo-Saxon.

The press and frustrations of papal business had made it necessary for Gregory to find some rest. He went, as he says at the beginning of the Dialogues, to a "quiet spot, congenial to my mind." He is joined by Peter the deacon, his favorite pupil and companion. Peter elicits and receives the confidences of his master, who tells him of his regret for not having opted for the solitary life, like so many saintly persons he knew.

Peter's curiosity is aroused. Has there really been, in the recent past, here in Italy, this flowering of holiness, authenticated by miracles? Peter wants to know, and the Pope obliges by recounting episodes without number in the best tradition of the golden legend. Gregory, however, tries to minimize the importance of the wonders he relates. To Peter's question, "How is it that we cannot find men or women of this type today?" Gregory replies, "I believe there still are many such people in the world. One cannot conclude that there are no great saints just because no great miracles are worked. The true estimate of life, after all, lies in acts of virtue, not in the display of miracles. There are many, Peter, who without performing miracles are not at all inferior to those who perform them" (D, I, 12).

Book II of St. Gregory's Dialogues is not a life of St. Benedict in the strict sense. Too many facts are missing. It is a spiritual portrait whose features are designed to offer a message, a doctrine. In recounting the miracles chosen from among others, the Pope intends to exemplify the qualities that make the saint, the spiritual person. But St. Gregory did not invent what he narrates. He worked on preexistent material received from witnesses who could testify firsthand to the life of St. Benedict. True, he discarded what was not directly to his purpose, and the Dialogues consequently are a work tailored to a thesis, but a thesis that purports to rest on concrete facts. That the facts were poorly verified by St. Gregory, or that he was perhaps too inclined to accept reports of the spectacular in regard to God's power, this no one doubts. Nevertheless, the reports did exist. If St. Benedict had a legend, it was not manufactured by St. Gregory; nor is a young legend likely to be without foundation.

The Rule

As books go, the Rule is a diminutive, an hour's reading, if that. St. Gregory's biography of the Abbot of Monte Cassino at best doubles the dossier at one's disposal. With only a legislative document, necessarily impersonal, to go by and a biography more indicative of Pope Gregory's mind than his subject's, what are the chances of discovering the inner truth, the soul of what Benedict believed? It seems like attempting the impossible. Benedict of Nursia never refers to his personal relations with his God. He left no spiritual diary, no "confessions" to bare his soul. His concern was to organize the common monastic life; to define the complex patterns of relationships and duties that touched every member of his claustral family, and to propound the practices that would serve them in their quest of God.

God is present throughout the Rule. Not that the Rule is a treatise on God or his mysteries, but God dominates the Rule by constant reference to him as terminus of the disciple's spiritual journey. The terminus, however, is not treated in and for itself.

Fortunately for our purpose, no code of Christian antiquity is simply a legislative document, juridical and impersonal through and through. "Rule" is a name with many connotations. Monks regarded the Bible as their first rule of life. The life of a saint, of a monastic founder, is a norm, a rule of life. Rule also applies to the living teaching of a spiritual master, of an abbot. As for Rules in the proper sense, they are very rich documents. In addition to particular and nonessential prescriptions, they contain exhortations, counsels, and especially universal teachings. They bear the mark of a long process of elaboration that they both reflect and consolidate.

St. Benedict's Rule is a masterpiece. It excels by far all the Latin Rules of his time. It lays down general rules and principles, clear, magnanimous and flexible, evidence of his own rich experience. Its exhortations are well considered and to the point. Though concerned for balance and moderation, it is careful not to stifle any generous impulse, but at the same time displays great practical wisdom. It has been aptly compared to a clear, bright fire, glowing rather than ablaze. It possesses a quality truly its own, very pure, as though distilled.

The Dialogues portray a hermit who became a spiritual father despite himself, a mystic endowed with many charismatic gifts: the gift of tears, of special knowledge of God and secrets of the heart, the gift of miracles. The Rule projects a sage: a wise and prudent lawgiver for a monachism formed of moderation and discretion.

The Problem of Sources

St. Benedict is no exception to lawgivers in every age. His work utilizes older sources. He refers to Scripture most of all, and in its own words. His Rule, as we shall see, tries to make the scriptural message real, to weave it into the daily life of his followers. In the final chapter St. Benedict recommends to the person "who would hasten to the perfection of [religious] life the teachings of the holy Fathers. . . . For what book of the holy Catholic Fathers does not loudly proclaim how we may come by a straight course to our Creator? Then the Conferences and the Institutes[2] and the Lives of the Fathers, as also the Rule of our holy father Basil — what else are they but tools of virtue for right-living and obedient monks?" (R 73) [3]

The works he recommends to his followers Benedict himself had read, meditated on, and absorbed. He had no intention of producing an original work. Hence, he did not scruple to draw extensively from the books of his predecessors, the common treasure of the monastic tradition. Many passages of his Rule make implicit reference to the Church Fathers: St. Augustine especially, but also St. Ambrose, St. Jerome and St. Leo the Great. There are numerous undertones of St. Cyprian, others of Sulpicius Severus (in his Life of St. Martin). There are echoes of liturgical sources, the Gelasian Sacramentary in particular.

As for monastic authors, St. Benedict's considerable indebtedness to Cassian has long been recognized. But Cassian is not the only monastic author to appear in the Rule. Also encountered are borrowings from such non-Western sources as the Rule of St. Pachomius, of St. Basil, the *Regula Patrum* and the *Regula Orientalis* attributed to St. Macarius, and collections of apothegms[4] known in a translation made in Rome by Pelagius and John at the time of St. Benedict. Additionally, there are the perennial Lives of the Fathers, the Lausiac History of Palladius, and Rufinus' History of Monks. Rules of Western provenance also are drawn upon: the Rules of St. Augustine and that of St. Caesarius of Arles.

The whole Egyptian and Eastern tradition makes its influence felt through Cassian, who inspired the doctrinal chapters of the Rule. To some extent the Rule has the appearance of patchwork, a sewing of excerpts. But this comes from the nature of the Rule. Like other works of its kind, it necessarily incorporates a variety of elements common to all monachism.

Commentators consequently have long been busy identifying

---

[2] The Conferences and the Institutes are works of John Cassian (d. 440), the principal source for Western monks of the monastic traditions of Egypt.

[3] *St. Benedict's Rule for Monasteries*, trans. Leonard J. Doyle (Collegeville, Minnesota: The Liturgical Press, 1948).

The letter R and the number stand for the *Rule of St. Benedict* and the chapter.

[4] A Greek derivative denoting a precept, a pointed saying, a didactic maxim with incisive meaning. The collections of apothegms reflect the teaching of Egyptian and Palestinian monks.

St. Benedict's borrowings and comparing them with parallel passages of the earlier monastic tradition, East and West. But no one, until rather recently, paid much attention to a very lengthy Rule, the most prolix by far of all the Rules that have been preserved, and known through the "Concordance of Rules" produced by the Carolingian monk, Benedict of Aniane.[5] This diffuse work, copied out from the aforesaid "Concordance," consists of a very long prologue and ninety-five chapters, most of them quite copious. Many passages are common with the Rule of St. Benedict, especially in its first chapters.

It is a commonly accepted canon of textual criticism that the presumption of priority goes to the shorter version. The profuseness of Aniane's "Rule," which also suffers from a lack of coherence, quickly led to its acceptance as the first known commentary on the Rule of St. Benedict. The Carolingian monk titled his document *Rule of the Master*. Actually, its text is completely anonymous. Some manuscripts designate it *Rule of the Fathers*, without further identification.

Shortly before the first World War a monk of Solesmes, Dom Augustine Genestout, who was preparing a new critical edition of St. Benedict's Rule, decided to take a closer look at the passages common to both Rules. The upshot of his analysis was the announcement that the traditional view of interdependence is incorrect. St. Benedict, he contended, was the debtor and appropriated parts of the Master. The situation was now reversed: the Master was not a commentator of St. Benedict; rather, it was the Patriarch of monks who figured as abridger and disciple.

Understandably, Dom Genestout's revolutionary thesis was immediately challenged, the more so because a number of weak points did militate against it. Still, after thirty-five years of discussion and critical research; after two international congresses, one at Spoleto in 1956, the other in Rome in 1971; after the integral edition of the Rule of the Master and minute analyses, historical, theological and philological, the priority of the Rule of the Master is a hypothesis decidedly more probable than the reverse.

But the story of the Rule of the Master is still only in its beginning. The Rule has undergone several recensions, and the primitive

---

[5] In an effort to produce a sort of commentary on St. Benedict's Rule, Benedict of Aniane (750–821) assembled parallel passages from early monastic rules of his acquaintance.

text is not available. Is it the work of several successive authors, or only of one? At what stage of its redaction does the connection with the Rule of St. Benedict appear? Did the Benedictine Rule influence the final redaction of the Rule of the Master, as some internal evidence seems to suggest? These are so many questions that are still without satisfactory answer and are likely to remain so for a long time to come. The earliest known manuscript of the Rule of the Master is a half century later than the first appearance of the Benedictine Rule.

Whatever the future may bring, the experience gained from the work of biblical exegesis should be a warning against oversimplification of the issue. It is not absolutely certain that the text of the Master is a homogeneous whole in style or that it is inspired by one dominant purpose and is the work of a single author. A monastic rule, the fruit of experience, generally develops in stages; founders of more recent orders have taught us that. The gestation is necessarily slow. The first developments are subsequently revised and amended, glossed and annotated, or simply added to, all with an eye to improvement or as daily needs require. Attempts at revision or achieving consistency do not necessarily correct every minor incoherence. Nor did a celebrated author have to die before copies of his work were made. Nor was revision itself reserved for his survivors. The author himself might go back over his work, touching it up till the day of his death. Many anomalies are thus accounted for.

Finally, it is important to distinguish between the literary sources themselves and the particular use made of them. The author of a Rule is an abbot who himself had received a spiritual formation within a living tradition. His very office gained him a personal experience all his own. When he makes use of an earlier work he does not become its slave or necessarily adopt every aspect of it, even when taking over long excerpts word for word. He incorporates in his personal work the fruit of his reading. As a result, borrowings he makes from a pre-existent codex are transformed and bear his mark. Benedict is far more personal than appears to the superficial reader. His Rule is truly his.

The Rule, "quintessence of perfection"

The Rule of the Master organized the life of the monastery and its ascetical practice around the person of the abbot. St. Benedict does not set aside this basic conception but completes it with the new dimensions of brotherly relations, mutual regard, and charity. Here

St. Augustine, ignored or unknown by the Master, is his guide and point of reference. The Augustinian influence again is seen when it is left to the living authority of the abbot to deal with many concrete details for which Benedict, unlike the Master, declines to draw up binding rules.

Benedict displays a rare understanding of persons and circumstances, an evolution toward a more remedial and pastoral view of authority. In general, the Abbot of Monte Cassino focuses on the subjective and qualitative aspect of observance and, through numerous reminders, puts the emphasis on the central element of monastic life: charity. Souls are his major preoccupation. He is attentive to the needs of the weak, to those who are experiencing difficulty or are given to discouragement. But he can also be strict, and is sometimes more severe than the Master.

He entertains no penitential practices except fasting, abstinence, and the Vigils (night Office); and he wants them moderate. Much is left to the individual discretion and generosity, under the watchful care of the abbot. Austerity is real but not crushing. Work occupies a large place, and St. Benedict does not hesitate to shorten the Office at times because of work.

He did not write a doctrinal treatise for his disciples but a legislative code. He offers a practical means of realizing the very high ideal set forth by Cassian in the Conferences, and characterizes his work as "this minimum Rule, written for beginners" (R 73). To him it is an introduction, a point of departure. Its purpose is to prepare the soul for the highest contemplation; to mark out the path of onward ascetical practice that leads to pure prayer in the Holy Spirit, when no barriers remain and the soul is at last open to the illimitable action of the third Person of the Trinity: the attainment of "the loftier heights of doctrine and virtue" (R 73).

The Rule is a kind of synthesis bringing together the spiritual teaching of monastic forms and traditions that preceded it: Egypt, St. Basil, St. Augustine. Partly through the Master, Benedict was able to reduce these multiple contributions to an integrated whole. Gregory the Great, thinking primarily of the Old Testament prophets and the apostles, describes him as "filled with the spirit of all the just"; to which one might add, without exaggeration, the spirit of the fathers of monachism as well. Benedict's Rule profited from the experience and the charismatic gifts of all the ancients; it retained what was best and had most proved itself. By the goal it sets itself and by the *discretio* (in the sense of "discernment of spirits") that governs it, the Rule qualifies as a complete recapitulation of the practical evangelical ideal of perfection, lived and exemplified in monastic community.

According to St. Benedict of Cluse, the Rule contains "all evangelical and apostolic perfection."[6] History confirms this judgment. It would be a mistake to see it only as a stage in an evolution still in process. No doubt it is that in a number of its practical provisions, now obsolete. There is room, yes need, for constant adaptation and, in some areas, for greater precision. But the doctrinal parts that predominate and form the bedrock of Benedictinism are of permanent value.

"You ask me what I think," wrote a mystic of the seventeenth century, Marie of the Incarnation. "My reply is that the quintessence of perfection is contained [in this Rule]. There is no Order in the Church that does not owe its most sacred endowments to St. Benedict and his saintly sons and daughters."[7]

---

[6] *Vita,* n. 4, *Monumenta Germaniae Historica, Scriptorum,* XII (Hanover, 1856), 199.

[7] *Correspondence,* Letter 81 (1644), Solesmes, 1971, 228.

2

Character Sketch of St. Benedict of Nursia

Ever since Andrea de Cione Orcagna, a fourteenth century painter (d. ca. 1368), St. Benedict has been depicted rod in hand. Nothing is more apt to turn off people of the twentieth century. Benedict of Nursia knew the use of corporal punishment — could it have been otherwise for a contemporary of the first Merovingian kings? — but the trend set by the Tuscan painter limits the image of the abbot in the extreme and falsifies it. Benedict was neither a pedagogue in charge of juveniles of arrested development, nor an armed policeman enforcing respect for the law. His pastoral staff has a completely different meaning.

But the question persists. Why does Benedict appear so austere at first acquaintance, when in fact he was the soul of kindness and condescension personified? He suffered with the suffering, loved everyone, was indulgent to a fault (except with pride), and unwilling that anyone around him should be sad.

Partly responsible is the iconography, especially of modern times. The St. Benedicts of the Beuronese school, with their Olympian stiffness, their beards and their tomes, are not particularly inviting. Gregory the Great's portrayal of the Abbot of Cassino also had its repercussions on his image. Despite the charm of the

11

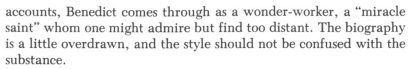

accounts, Benedict comes through as a wonder-worker, a "miracle saint" whom one might admire but find too distant. The biography is a little overdrawn, and the style should not be confused with the substance.

The Human Qualities

Unpleasant temperaments do not attract, even when redeemed by close union with God. Benedict of Nursia enjoyed a great attraction among his contemporaries. He had the gift of evoking affection, and appears to have been a very likable person. His nurse loved him enough to follow him to his first retreat. His first miracle, that of mending for his nurse the broken tray, shows that he could enter into and understand the suffering of others: "Benedict, who had always been a devout and thoughtful boy, felt sorry for his nurse when he saw her weeping" (D 1). After the tray was mended, Gregory shows the young ascetic "cheerfully reassuring" her.

The attachment of the monk Romanus is similarly explained, attracted as he was from their first meeting. Benedict's personality radiated charm, and it drew him disciples, monks, even laypeople, like the brother of the monk Valentinian "who visited the abbey every year to get Benedict's blessing and see his brother" (D 13).

Though he had the gift of winning the heart, Benedict did not pride himself on it. He was, first and last, a man of poise, with a penchant for orderliness that he loved to see around him. His idea of the follower was that of a well-ordered person, composed, mature, and of solid character. He loves administrators who know what they are doing and do not neglect their office. He wants practical arrangements to be trimmed to the realities of monastic life.

Not that he is overly meticulous or picayunish. In many ways, in fact, he is quite liberal and flexible, but nothing offends him more than gossip mongers, or disciples who are indifferent, squander time and the community's goods and in general show a lack of foresight. When these faults become a way of life, as with vagabond monks (St. Benedict calls them "gyrovagues") or with monks without a superior (whom he calls "sarabaites"), he does not find words strong enough to castigate them: "a detestable kind . . . of whose miserable conduct it is better to be silent than to speak" (R 1). St. Benedict wants his followers to cultivate order; he prescribes inventories in order to know what comes in and what goes out. Both work and reading are to be regular occupations, conscientiously pursued.

Serious is not synonymous with boring; seriousness is rather a sign of maturity. In some remarks of St. Benedict there is a distinct note of irritation at the profusion of words. Himself of earnest mold, he had little patience with frivolous and mischievous behavior. For all that, he is not a kill-joy, on more than one occasion betraying a sense of humor. But he does not want decisions made arbitrarily and without preparation. What he loves is a certain gravity of behavior, harnessed energy, silence, kindliness and mutual respect; above all, attentiveness to things monastic. Benedict strives for the right measure in everything, does nothing too hurriedly, takes time to reflect, looks for the balanced solution to a problem, one that will serve not only for the moment but promises to last. He has a predilection for souls who live in the deeper regions of the heart, not on the surface. He prizes silence, reveres peacefulness.

Prominent among his instruments of good works are the simple, natural virtues. Great value is placed on caring, on cleanliness and punctuality. Candidness, honesty, loyalty, temperance, the sense of responsibility, these are admired and inculcated. A life modulated by hours, days, seasons, and feasts was ideally suited to him — everything in its place. From the outset he was determined to ban certain practices which to him were the antithesis of monastic life. Accordingly, he locates his followers in a definite place, holds them there by the vow of stability and assigns them work, preferably according to their aptitudes and tastes. His monastery forms part of the countryside; it is rooted in the soil. But at the same time unlimited spiritual horizons open to the disciples whom he has gathered for an inner pilgrimage totally spiritual. Everything in their earthly habitation is sacred because God is in their midst.

This, then, is Benedict, a man without complication, practical and direct. He was not speculatively inclined but rather, in the highest degree, had a sense of the concrete, the world of reality. Instead of teachings learnedly expounded, he preferred description of attitudes and actions whose meaning was accessible to all. He also had a genius for the simple, lapidary phrase that is more easily remembered. Often he reminds one of the desert fathers with their "sentences" or "apothegms."

Another mark of his character was his regard for the truth and the logic of things: "An abbot who is worthy to be over a monastery should always remember what he is called, and live up to the name of Superior" (R 2). "Let the oratory be what it is called, a place of prayer; and let nothing else be done there or kept there" (R 52). The monk has no other program than to fulfill the vocation inscribed in his name. What he is and what he does should correspond. His entire life is to be an effort toward eliminating the contradictions and failures of truth that discredit so many of us.

The language of St. Benedict is the language of his time. He speaks simply to simple people in the Latin of Campanians in the sixth century. His style is brisk, fluent, and utterly innocent of studied elegance. The idea of producing a literary work never crossed his mind. He was not averse to repeating himself, and throughout the Rule the same words, the same expressions recur again and again. This guarantees the homogeneity of the whole, the single authorship of all the parts despite a certain disorder in the composition. Nevertheless, Benedict has the qualities of a real author: he explains and clarifies his literary borrowings, and sometimes just a minor touch illuminates an obscure passage of his predecessors.

Benedict writes spontaneously. Certain expressions seem to echo his oral teaching, words he loved to repeat to his followers. There are stereotyped locutions, and ideas untiringly pressed. Like the Evangelist St. John, who is cited sparingly, he seems unaware of repeating himself. Sentence after sentence, he goes back over his thought, refining and completing it with this or that nuance. He proceeds in this way throughout his Rule.

Were these repetitions truly unconscious? Repetition favors memorization. In the case of St. Benedict's disciples, maxims of the Rule were impressed upon their minds and recalled in their frequent meditation, producing in time reflex behavior conformed to affirmed principles.

Yet for all his repetition, Benedict of Nursia was not dull and unimaginative or locked into a sort of legalism. he had a perceptive mind with a keen sense of the finer distinctions in life and a promptitude for things of the spirit that transcend sheer reason. St. Benedict is intuitive. His sensibility to differences of age, origin, and social condition was extraordinary. He knows that natures are not alike and do not react alike. He shows concern for these differences and a readiness to adapt to them. In the chapter on drink he writes, "'Everyone has his own gift from God, one in this way and another in that' (1 Cor 7:7). It is therefore with some misgiving that we regulate the measure of other men's sustenance" (R 40). He does it, nonetheless; as abbot and lawgiver it was his duty.

The same consideration is evident in the legislation on work, sleep, the manner of correction, and the spiritual formation of his followers. He has regard for the "needs of weaker brethren" (R 40). The abbot must be on guard both against distinction of persons and the temptation to impose stubborn uniformity, so convenient to a leader. He must adapt himself to circumstances, "threatening at one time and coaxing at another as the occasion may require, showing now the stern countenance of a master, now the loving affection of a father" (R 2). The needs of each are not identical, but before God each is essentially equal and the same.

Benedict understands the weakness of human nature and has no illusions on that score. He knows that complaints may not be gratuitous, but he abhors grumbling ("the vice of murmurers") and tries to forestall it by removing the cause and even the pretext. He is aware of crises of discouragement when assigned work is too heavy (or imagined to be); and he knows of the temptation to flee the monastery. The Dialogues of Gregory do not reveal a community of pure spirits in the last stage of evangelical perfection. Surrounding the founder are gossips, gourmands, egotists; others cannot stay with the brethren at prayer time; obedience is far from being always satisfactory; there are even grave perversions of the spirit of poverty. St. Benedict's Rule shows him a realist: he does not demand too much; he takes precautions; he appeals to the supernatural in his disciples without falling into a supernaturalism that is blind and insensitive to weaknesses.

The founder is mindful of the effects of age on the psyche, of its mental and physical encroachments. He is not surprised that the generation gap among his followers poses problems and calls for careful handling. There are no illusions with him and no despair, only confidence and healthy optimism.

To round out this human portrait, attention should be called to the graciousness of St. Benedict. Many passages of the Dialogues give evidence of it. He is thankful even when handed poisoned bread, thankful when brought a donation half of which was withheld by the bearer. He had the ability to read the human heart, but instead of squashing an exposed offender he makes a friendly remark or at worst a mild reproach, half in sorrow. Rarely does he show anger. It happens, but then he prays for his offender and gains him inwardly. He is kind and considerate without being weak, and when on occasion he must be severe, he is not harsh or intemperate. The secret of such inner harmony lies not only in the nature with which he was blessed; its source is in the holiness of Benedict.

Man of Faith

It was natural for the founder, considering his moral and spiritual fiber, to be an adamant defender of Christian orthodoxy. We shall have occasion to speak of his opposition to Pelagianism[1] and his strong reaction to the Arianism[2] of the Goths, invaders of Italy. In the Office he wants readings only from the canonical books of sacred Scripture and from "the explanations of them which have been made by well known and orthodox Catholic Fathers" (R 9). The same provision appears in chapter 73. There is to be no doubtful doctrine, only wholesome nurture for souls.

But this is just one aspect of his faith. To Benedict faith is a supreme value, first in importance and an indispensable condition for the whole monastic life. In many respects his career parallels that of Abraham, "who believed God." Bossuet in his panegyric of the Patriarch of monks addresses himself to the similarity. A first exodus took him from his father's house into the wilds. He abandons what he seems to possess in favor of the unknown to which he feels himself called. For love of God he was willing to venture his life in the eremitic enterprise. His first failure with the monks at Vicovaro did not dishearten him.

He also knew partial failure at Subiaco where his goodness and amiability were not enough to overcome the antagonism of the priest Florentius. To forestall the worst, he agreed to withdraw, trusting in God to bring to fruition the work begun.

At Monte Cassino he again set to work. He built a solid monastic community for which he wrote a Rule. But dark clouds loomed, as told by the saint to Theoprobus, whom he himself had converted to the monastic life: "One day on entering Benedict's room he found him weeping bitterly. After he had waited for some time and there was still no end to the abbot's tears, he asked what was causing him such sorrow, for he was not weeping as he usually did at prayer but with deep sighs and lamentations. 'Almighty God has decreed that this entire monastery and everything I have provided for the community shall fall into the hands of the barbarians,' the saint replied" (D 17).

---

[1] The Celtic monk Pelagius (fifth century) tended to exaggerate the role of the individual in the work of one's sanctification and return to God. For him grace primarily was an extrinsic enlightenment rather than an interior power elevating human action to the supernatural level.

[2] Arius (255–338), an Alexandrian priest, denied the equality of nature between the Son of God and his Father. For him, the Word was created and was not God in the true sense.

It now seemed to Benedict that his lifework would be a failure, doomed as it was to destruction. Monte Cassino was indeed destroyed in 589 by the Lombards. To test Benedict's faith God demanded of him the sacrifice of what he had toiled so long and hard to build. It is not recorded that God also revealed to him the future of his Order: barbarian Europe formed and transformed by the Rule of Cassino, and Benedict's patronage invoked on the nations of the West. Like Abraham, St. Benedict lived by faith, accepting loss after loss and the sacrifice of what was dearest to him, yet always sure of God's faithfulness, no matter what. His trust was absolute.

For the sanctification of his disciples Benedict did not rely on his Rule, or the observances he laid down, or any human strength, but on God alone. The work to be accomplished was God's work; God was its author and finisher, and despite appearances it was being realized through the weakness of human means.

Because he had faith, St. Benedict was a man of prayer. He was constantly aware of the divine presence and asked his followers to keep themselves in this presence as though it were visible. Seriousness of purpose and inner recollection shone in his demeanor. The Abbot of Monte Cassino was a man with whom God alone mattered. The thought of God was his guiding light and oriented him to the invisible, to the face of the Lord. His soul was not completely itself except in the conscious practice of this relationship of dependence. It rejoiced in the protective hand of the Almighty. Seeking after God was its one desire, arising from deep within itself like an innate thrust, powerful yet tranquil, that turned it upward toward its Creator. "All creation," comments St. Gregory, "is bound to appear small to a soul that sees the Creator. Once it beholds a little of his light, it finds all creatures small indeed. The light of holy contemplation enlarges and expands the mind in God until it stands above the world" (D 35).

The fruits of this inner steadfastness were peace and joy. St. Benedict likes to see his sons and daughters happy; he wants "no one to be troubled or vexed in the house of God" (R 31).

Several of his miracles had no other purpose than to bring peace and contentment to those around him. The miracle of the iron blade retrieved from the lake is one. Benedict handed the tool back to the Goth and told him, "Continue with your work now. There is no need to be upset" (D 6).

Benedict, who taught his disciples to seek peace and pursue it (R Prol; Ps 33:15), did not let his own peace forsake him. He lived in a world in turmoil and had premonitions of still greater turmoil. It caused him sorrow, but it did not stop him from putting his trust in God. At the death of his sister he disregarded his personal loss and, his thoughts on what man does not see, was "overjoyed for her eternal glory, and gave thanks to God in hymns of praise" (D 34). God alone counted. It is strictly from this standpoint that he judges all things; hence the absolute primacy of the spiritual in the organization of his monastery and the consciousness of his own unimportance.

An Ardent Soul

Faith and humility: two qualities of the soul that Benedict rightly considered indispensable. Thanks to them he felt himself strong with the strength of God. He shows a stalwart character, resolute and persevering. His principles are firmly maintained, sometimes to the point of near rigidity. Was his failure with the monks of Vicovaro due to an excess of youthful strictness? One is tempted to think so. At any rate, he seems never to have completely forgotten it, and we get the impression that he fears the lack of authority more than some of its excesses. He is not afraid that it might be exercised rigorously, and the ideal he sets forth is very demanding.

Many times, nevertheless, he takes into account the shortcomings and limitations of his people, superiors as well as subjects. He confronts these realities of life without being scandalized like the Pharisee or surprised like the master making the sad discovery of having counted too much on a disciple. His penal code is a masterpiece of human sensitivity. In Chapter 68 — "If a Brother is Commanded to Do Impossible Things," things that seem too difficult — he puts himself in the position of the disciple under obedience and permits him to state his case. But he does not, in truth, retreat from any of his demands or consent to a reduction of the ideal.

In the case of St. Benedict, perhaps more than in others, appearances can be deceiving. Behind the tranquil exterior, behind the prudent, practical, and seemingly ordinary manner, and the good-naturedness worthy of a St. Francis de Sales, he concealed a devouring fire, an insatiable thirst for perfection. An interior life of incredible force impelled him. This tolerant, kindly, illusionless leader could not be content with mediocrity. He wants no half measure in the spiritual life. There is in him a kind of compulsion, a drive for absoluteness. In his view life is not worth living unless it strives for the perfection of love. In this he is uncompromising and does not yield until unity of purpose and resolve has been achieved; until, that is, the struggle between the forces of good and evil has been won. The purity of his desire is absolute. He wants his disciples to give all on earth, in order to gain all in heaven. Not only the message but the vocabulary also proclaims his thirst, his ardor. He loves superlatives, expressions of totality and exclusion: "always, never, all, absolutely no one, in no case, at once, in all respects, by every means."

This ardor overflows in charity, commiseration, and sympathetic understanding. Many of his miracles, as we have said, are prompted by the desire to relieve distress or want. He condoles with the grieved, with the anguished; he comforts (D 27), he listens, he opens his heart, and in the Rule, though he may seem the master, he is foremost the very loving father.

Such is the author of the Rule: a force thoroughly master of itself, humbly regardful of God's absolute rights and prepared to sacrifice his all for them. Now and then an abbot or a monk is said to be "another Benedict." This is high praise indeed, but it only underscores the exceptional importance of the first Benedict in the history of the spiritual life. A beautiful antiphon of Germanic origin names him *caelestis norma vitae*, a difficult title to translate but one that calls to mind the idea of a living rule and a model of the angelic life. The antiphon also bestows on St. Benedict the titles of "doctor" and "leader." This he is even today, enduringly, after fifteen hundred years.

3

the Word of God

St. Benedict knew the Scriptures thoroughly. Copious references with implicit and explicit citations demonstrate his familiarity with God's word. There is no doubt that he himself lent it the attentive hearing that he wants in his disciples: "Listen, my son" (R Prol), or that he "inclined the ear of his heart" to it. He tried to make this hearing easier for his followers; there are several indications to this effect. During the readings in the Office, which were mostly from the inspired books recognized as such by the Church (books of divine authority), the community assumed a more comfortable position: they sat, whereas for the psalms they stood. In the refectory, where readings left unfinished in choir were continued, "let absolute silence be kept, so that no whispering may be heard nor any voice except the reader's" (R 38).

Not everyone was reader. Chosen were those with the ability to be heard and to profit the listeners: "The brethren are not to read in order, but only those who edify their hearers" (R 38).

The brethren had many occasions to read or hear the Scriptures. The night Office included long readings, from three to twelve, depending on the day or season. At table they again heard it, and for Compline they came together to listen to some four or five manuscript pages. Frequently between the night and morning Office time was spent on the Scriptures, with memorization of long passages that would be recalled and dwelled upon during work. In addition, there were the hours devoted to *lectio divina*, that meditative reading of which Scripture was the major part, together with commentaries by the holy Fathers. Thus, by will of the lawgiver and abbot Benedict, who was only following a long monastic tradition, the Bible is the pre-eminent book of the Benedictine, the only one that is truly studied for its own sake.

The Bible in the Rule

St. Benedict does not quote every book of the Bible. Special recognition is given to the psalms, which he knew by heart and so apportioned to the Office that all of them would be said in the course of every week. Certain ones, moreover, were to recur daily.

The sapiential books afforded him a wealth of short didactic sentences, easily remembered, that found a natural place in a Rule whose tone is reminiscent of biblical wisdom literature: "Receive willingly and carry out effectively your loving father's advice" (R Prol). Sirach and Proverbs are also often cited.

Since Benedict's purpose was to outline a way to contemplative prayer through practices of the spiritual combat that are presupposed (the *ascesis*), he looks principally to the Gospel of St. Matthew for his moral teaching. He also draws upon the moral portions of St. Paul's epistles, rather than the strictly doctrinal content.

In an effort to lead his disciples to conversion and to encourage them and support their pursuit of the virtuous life, Benedict gives the example of a variety of biblical figures: Jacob, Samuel, Daniel, the high priest Heli, St. Paul, Ananias and Sapphira. He chose persons who had or had not practiced what the Scriptures call "fear of the Lord," an interior attitude including attention to God, reverence, and humility inspired by love. Sometimes monastic observances are reinforced by scriptural allusions or formal citations. Seldom does he fail to provide biblical ground and justification for whatever he proposes.

The meaning he gives to certain passages of the Bible might not be that of the modern exegete. But Benedict does not pose as an exegete; his intention was to give scriptural dress to his own thought and scriptural footing to the monastic life he and his followers were leading. He chose passages that seemed most apt and skillfully wove them into the context. He may make a simple accommodation of a text or adopt an allegorical interpretation of the sort that others before him had used as a theme for the spiritual life (e.g., Jacob's ladder and the degrees of humility). But the basic reason for whatever liberty he takes was to make understandable to the disciples of his time what God was saying to them.

God Calling: Here and Now

For Benedict the Bible was not simply a book of reference or an object of study. What he sought and found there was a message of the present, a call heard here and now.

In this respect the ancient monks and nuns had something of an advantage: to them the Bible was a book heard rather than read. Monasteries and convents had each a very limited number of works. Seldom would one find several copies of the Bible, except for certain parts like the Psalter and the Gospels. It was mostly through public reading (through the ear) that God's message gained entrance to the soul, with the character of a living and direct call. When, in addition, followers of Benedict read privately, they did more than run their eyes over the page; they literally read it to themselves in muted voice yet loud enough to hear themselves read the word of God much as one reads a poem for full effect. Among the instruments of good works Benedict places "to listen willingly to holy reading" (R 4). Elsewhere he speaks of the divine voice and the divine discourse (*eloquium*).

Scripture consequently assumed the actuality of a message spoken *this* day to *this* disciple. It had the impact of a book just off the press. Materially it was in the position of a work of music that exists anew in a manner utterly unique each time it is performed.

Reading technique, however, is not enough to explain the transforming presence and power of God's word. God, who is eternally and inwardly present to every action of his temporal creature, is singularly present whenever Scripture is proclaimed. The Holy Spirit, received in baptism, indwells the soul, prepares it for God's seed, and works beforehand to open the ears of the heart to his word. The "cry" of Scripture (R 7) is perceived as the voice, the call of God. The call is heard, and the soul embraces it as a personal message with its living demands addressed to it individually. The Lord was not satisfied to speak only in the past; today he still lifts his voice. His word is not a static reality, lying inert between the covers of a book. It is what it is called, a word, that is to say, the manifestation of a living person whom one recognizes by the tone of voice.

Before it even grasps the content of the message, the heart is touched and drawn to the beloved.

"Let us open our eyes to the deifying light, let us hear with attentive ears the warning which the divine voice cries daily to us, 'Today if you hear his voice, harden not your hearts' (Ps 94:8). And again, 'He who has ears to hear, let him hear what the Spirit says to the churches' (Rev 2:7)" (R Prol).

"The Lord, seeking his laborer in the multitude to whom he thus cries out, says again, 'Who is the one who will have life, and desires to see good days?'" (*Ibid.*, see Ps 34:13)

"What can be sweeter to us, dear brethren, than this voice of the Lord inviting us? Behold, in his loving kindness the Lord shows us the way of life" (*Ibid.*).

It is not only out of the distant past that God's call is heard; it is today that he comes to elicit a response from us and engage in dialogue.

The Rule and the Gospel

St. Benedict calls the disciple to the school of the gospel: "Let us walk in the paths of the Lord by the guidance of the gospel" (R Prol). By these words the Father of monks expresses his intention to establish a life patterned after the gospel. This is the only true foundation on which a community rests. St. Benedict was well aware that his work represented an embodiment of the gospel designed for his followers, and Bossuet saw in the Rule "a learned and surprising digest of the entire gospel teaching."[1]

The gospel is the reference point by which to judge the ordinances of the Rule. It is the key to the spirit, to the particular genius of the Rule and the rationale behind the way it organizes monastic life. It is the supreme norm, and the abbot has no other task than to see that the life of his monks conforms to it: "The abbot ought not to teach or ordain or command anything which is against the Lord's precepts; on the contrary, his commands and his teaching should be a leaven of divine justice kneaded into the minds of his disciples" (R 2).

There is scarcely an observance in Benedict's monastery that does not have at least implicit reference to the gospel and is based on it. If Scripture and its commentaries are read at table, it is because the Lord said, "Man shall not live by bread alone, but by every word

---

[1] Bossuet, *Panegyric of St. Benedict*, 1665; ed. J. LeBarcq, IV (Paris, n.d.), 630.

that proceeds from the mouth of God" (Matt 4:4). The entire chapter on humility is governed by its first statement: "Holy Scripture, brethren, cries out to us, saying, 'Everyone who exalts himself shall be humbled, and he who humbles himself shall be exalted'" (Luke 14:11; R 7). Christ is the master and the teacher, and the community the school where he teaches: "Learn from me; for I am gentle and lowly in heart," an explicit citation of the Lord (Matt 11:29). This is the reason for coming to the school of the Lord's service—to learn humility and gentleness of heart.

For St. Benedict, sacred Scripture has one author. When he speaks of the words of the Lord, he has in mind not only the New Testament *logia*.[2] The message of the Eternal Word of God is not limited to the very words of Christ, the *ipsissima verba*, words certainly authentic in the form they assumed on the lips of the Redeemer in Aramaic. The words of Christ are found throughout Scripture, and it is one and the same Lord who speaks there, from end to end.

In the Prologue, St. Benedict quotes freely from Psalm 34, which reads in part: "Who desires life and covets many days, that he may enjoy good? Keep your tongue from evil and your lips from speaking deceit. Depart from evil and do good" (vv. 13–14). He hears in these words Christ calling, and what his call entails. He exhorts the disciple to answer the call and conform to the gospel: "Having our loins girded, therefore, with faith and the performance of good works, let us walk in his paths by the guidance of the gospel . . ." (R Prol; see Eph 6:14-15). Similarly, his paraphrase of Psalm 14 is accommodated to the gospel, Matt 7:24-25.

In meditating on the Old Testament, St. Benedict makes the transfer to the gospel as a matter of course. He projects the light of the gospel on the entire word of God and gives it a Christian reading.

Lectio divina

Occupation with the word of God can take the form of meditative prayer: such was *lectio divina*. It was reading done alone, in private. St. Benedict clearly provided for this use of the disciple's time, but to those incapable of applying themselves to it he has some light work assigned instead. Though private, the reading was not

---

[2] *logia:* the utterances or teachings attributed to Christ and recorded in the gospels or in other writings of the apostolic age.

altogether unsupervised: "One or two of the seniors should be deputed to go about the monastery at the hours when the brethren are occupied in reading and see that there be no lazy brother who spends his time in idleness or gossip and does not apply himself to the reading, so that he is not only unprofitable to himself but also distracts others" (R 48).

This piece of inside information on monastic behavior suggests that St. Benedict allowed his followers considerable latitude as to the place of reading. It could be the oratory, the cloister, the dormitory, the garden. Benedict himself preferred the entrance to the monastery, which overlooked a picturesque expanse stretching far and wide from the foot of Monte Cassino. An episode of the Dialogues shows him at his favorite spot: The Arian Goth named Zalla had been hounding Christians. One day he collared a peasant farmer and pummeled him for his money. The poor man, to gain time, protested that all his money was in Abbot Benedict's safekeeping. Whereupon Zalla bound his hands behind his back with a good strong rope and mounting his horse, "forced the farmer to walk ahead of him and lead the way to this Benedict who was keeping his money. . . . When they arrived, they found the man of God sitting alone in front of the entrance, reading." One glance from the abbot, and the prisoner's bonds fell to his feet. But neither the miracle nor the trembling Zalla's ensuing prostrations could divert Benedict from his reading (D 31).

The monks spent hours every day on the book given to them by direction of the abbot: "They shall each receive a book from the library, which they shall read straight through from the beginning. These books are to be given out at the beginning of Lent" (R 48).

It is possible, then, to distinguish three ways for St. Benedict's followers to come into contact with Scripture: 1) listening to scriptural readings at the night Office, in the refectory, at Compline; 2) studying and memorizing it in the morning after the night Office, as prescribed in the Rule: "The time that remains after the night Office should be spent in study by those brethren who need a better knowledge of the Psalter or the lessons" (R 8); 3) *lectio divina*, the unhurried, affective reading frequently interrupted by prayer, and for which several hours were set aside daily and all day Sunday and feast days except for the hours of the Office and special duties assigned to some. By force of circumstances—lack of copies, for one— *lectio divina* did not ordinarily come from sacred Scripture itself but from commentaries and the small patristic library to which St. Benedict refers in chapter 73 of the Rule.[3]

The reading was a sacred activity, *sacra lectio*. Its first and most important aim was not simply the acquisition of knowledge but a special kind of wisdom: knowledge with moral goodness or "fear of the Lord." All attention of mind and heart was fastened on the reading; the love and desire of God were nurtured as the author's message was gradually absorbed. In St. Benedict's Rule monastic reading is a prayed reading that leads to contemplation. Medieval writers spoke of "the prayer of meditation." The monk is alone with his book, alone before God. He has plenty of time to pause over a word, a thought, and can resume his reading as the soul inclines. He is much freer than when reading to the whole community or listening with the community. Consequently, his prayer takes a more spontaneous turn. Spiritually nourished by hearing the Scriptures read at other times, in *lectio divina* he again meets an author who speaks to him of God, much in the words of sacred Scripture, and through affective prayer he makes the message more securely his own, the better to live its content.

Practicing God's Word

It is not enough to hear, to read, even to love God's word. It must be put into practice, and imbue the disciple's life. St. Benedict is a firm believer in the efficacy of God's word. In the chapters on the correction of erring brethren he instructs the abbot to apply, among others, "the medicines of the Holy Scriptures" (R 28). He is convinced that the Scriptures have a latent power to soften the rebellious will and gently bring it round to observance of their teaching.

The word of God is implanted through faith and is an object of faith, but without the will's active cooperation it cannot grow and thoroughly christianize every corner of the disciple's life, especially the corners that have resisted its influence.

Chapter 4 in the Rule is devoted to the instruments of good works: phrases and sentences culled from the Bible or inspired by it. According to St. Benedict, this catalogue of spiritual precepts constitutes the disciple's tools or equipment provided by God to accomplish the good that attracted him or her to the monastery or convent in the first place.

---

[3] St. Benedict does not speak of spiritual conferences that certainly existed. Nor does he indicate how the community acquired the rudiments of education necessary for *lectio divina*.

Benedict pursues the comparison: "These, then, are the tools of the spiritual craft. If we employ them unceasingly day and night, and return them on the Day of Judgment, our compensation from the Lord will be that wage he has promised: 'Eye has not seen, nor ear heard what God has prepared for those who love him' (1 Cor 2:9). Now the workshop in which we shall diligently execute all these tasks is the enclosure of the monastery and stability in the community" (R 4).

Equipped with the word of God, the disciples of Benedict strive daily to put it to work in their lives. They are confident of its power and of God's strength to support them. They advance toward the light already dawning over the horizon.

4

the Love of God

In an Italy dominated by Arian Goths, Benedict of Nursia emphatically declared his belief in the Trinity. He gave particular expression to it in the very structure of the choir Office he adopted. But the whole life of his follower, as he envisaged it, is controlled by the presence and the action of the three divine Persons; one's whole life, then, should be lived accordingly.

The Father's love, preeminently shown in the Son, stirs the disciple's response of love through conformity to Christ and to the selfless charity of Christ by the working of the Holy Spirit. Generally the Rule focuses on the second stage of this itinerary. Yet the Rule necessarily presupposes the first and also makes frequent reference to the third, the terminus, especially in the chapter on humility and in the last two chapters of the Rule as well. The itinerary of the spiritual life begins with a revelation of love and ends in a very pure and perfect love of its source, the Father who produces it.

Judging from the Dialogues of Gregory, the first episodes in the life of St. Benedict are marked by a consciousness of the Father's love. This is the more noteworthy because Gregory mentions flight from a corrupt world as one of the motives that determined Benedict's eremetical vocation, a negative motive scarcely understood today.

The facts as reported in the Dialogues are well known. Benedict, already converted, lives at Affile, his nurse his only attendant. One day she borrows a tray for cleaning wheat and accidentally breaks it. The woman bursts into tears and will not be consoled. Benedict, helpless, has recourse to God, convinced that the Father's love was closer to the needs of his nurse than was his own (D 1). The human heart is an image of God's. If Benedict's heart was moved by the pain of his nurse, all the more was God's. The miracle of the tray bespeaks a child's trust in God's love and in his solicitous concern over every human distress, however small.

Becoming a hermit at Subiaco, Benedict lives unknown to the world. Only Romanus, a monk in the monastery of Abbot Deodatus, knew of his cave and supplied him with necessities. However, the effort seems to have cost him considerable physical fatigue. "The time came," notes Gregory, "when almighty God wished to grant Romanus rest from his toil." On this occasion God's love again takes the form of fatherly care: "The Lord therefore appeared in a vision to a priest some distance away who had just prepared his Easter dinner. 'How can you prepare these delicacies for yourself,' the Lord asked, 'while my servant is out there in the wilds suffering from hunger?'" (D 1) The "*my* servant" is revealing. God concerns himself personally with Benedict. A very intimate interpersonal relationship is attested.

Benedict, now Abbot of Monte Cassino, finds that at the center of every monastic vocation, which is the baptismal vocation extended, there is an experience similar to his. The monk discovers that God loves him with a personal love, stoops to him, and sounds an urgent call — something like the "Adam, where are you?" in the Book of Genesis (3:9).

God's love is uniquely manifested in Christ. Benedict uses the Prologue to speak about Christ to the candidate for the monastic life: about his prevenient love, his goodness, his mercy. These first pages of the Rule are an impressive declaration of the greatness of the love that flows from the heart of God.

God deigns to count us among his children. Our failure to act as such grieves him. He is Father and is deeply wounded when he sees no sign of love from his children. He came to seek us, that we might at last be persuaded to seek him. Though there is no explicit citation in the Rule from the Canticle of Canticles, one can hardly resist drawing a comparison when Benedict describes in such urgent tone God's call and search and what the disciple's response ought to be. This passage is especially to the point: "Hark! my beloved is knocking. 'Open to me, my sister, my love, . . . for my head is wet with dew, my locks with the drops of the night.' . . . I arose to open to my beloved; . . . I opened, . . . but my beloved had turned and gone. My soul failed me. . . . I sought him, but found him not; I called him, but he gave no answer" (Cant 5:2-6).

Similarly the disciple: the Lord seeks his laborer in the multitude, he makes his cry heard, and "what can be sweeter to us, dear brethren, than this voice of the Lord inviting us? Behold, in his loving kindness the Lord shows us the way of life" (R Prol). The Lord knocks; it is up to the disciple to answer and begin to seek the living God: "Having given us these assurances, the Lord is waiting every day for us to respond by our deeds to his holy admonitions. And the days of this life are lengthened and a truce granted us for this very reason, that we may amend our evil ways" (R Prol).

The Rule makes frequent use of the vocabulary of love. The Good Shepherd goes in search of his sheep; his love impels him, love that is anxious for the sheep, solicitous, and tender in its mercy. St. Benedict's concept of the abbot is modeled on our Lord. The abbot is the interpreter, the flesh and blood characterization of Christ's love for the disciple; he is a sort of sacrament of divine love that breathes life and warmth into all the Rule.

Faith and Trust in Love

"In all these things we are more than conquerors through him who loved us" (Rom 8:37). St. Benedict cites these words of St. Paul in the fourth degree of humility, the humility of heroic obedience under the most difficult and crucifying circumstances. The secret of the Christian's victories is faith in God's love. With the Abbot of Monte Cassino faith in the divine love was absolute. Whatever the circumstances, he put his trust in God. This trust was his peace. His soul was established in the serenity of peace, and it brought him the optimism of peace because he was convinced that God's enterprises do not fail but are crowned with supernatural success.

Benedict's peace did not leave him when the outlook was bleak, or only the worst was in sight. He hoped in God and asks his followers to do the same (R 4). But he means hope and trust that is total: the solid, never-failing anchor for the treacherous waters of this world, giving the soul a stability that nothing undermines. The Prologue proceeds from the certainty that God wants nothing more ardently than to give himself to the person in whom he arouses the desire for himself.

Yet on one occasion, according to St. Gregory, Benedict's sister Scholastica demonstrated a trust in love that was more absolute than his. The two had spent the whole day speaking of God and the things of God. Scholastica, overjoyed by this spiritual conversation, wanted it to continue: "Please do not leave me tonight, brother; let us keep on talking about the joys of heaven till morning." Benedict pleaded the demands of the Rule and said it was impossible. But that was not to be the end of it: "At her brother's refusal Scholastica folded her hands on the table and rested her head upon them in earnest prayer. When she looked up again, there was a sudden burst of lightning and thunder accompanied by such a downpour that Benedict and his companions were unable to set foot outside the door" (D 33).

Benedict loved his sister dearly, but he did not think he could make an exception for himself of a rule he asserted for his monks.[1] God showed him otherwise, and Scholastica could say, "When I appealed to you, you would not listen to me. So I turned to God and he heard my prayer" (*Ibid.*). She had thought, rightly, that God would be more lenient than Benedict and that his heart would understand. The Lord, the Almighty, put his power to use for the desire of his servant Scholastica, who had made an admirable act of faith in the actuality of his love.

The Disciple's Response

To the boundless love shown us and in which we put our trust, we respond with the gift of ourselves in the avowal of our love. On the day of profession the disciple intones: *Suscipe me*, "Receive me, O Lord, according to your word, and I shall live; and let me not be confounded in my hope" (Ps 119:116; R 58). Monastic life is a response to God's gift by the gift of ourselves. We surrender ourselves into the hands of the Lord in the realization that we would not be content anywhere else. We put implicit trust in God who loved us first, and abandon ourselves to God unconditionally. We no longer act from a sense of duty but from a need to express our love.

St. Benedict knows better than to suggest that his disciples have

---

[1] St. Benedict forbade his followers to be away from the monastery at night. If they were gone by day, they were expected to return before nightfall.

to attain perfection and complete selflessness before they can declare their love to God. He knows that deeds motivated by the charity of Christ are the most effective and expeditious means of gaining the purification that leads to the dominance of love.

Benedictines are members of God's family, sons and daughters. They work and obey as sons and daughters, with the love of family members. Love makes them more obedient than slaves, and without loss of human dignity; in fact, just the opposite. It is when they forsake love that they begin to become slaves. Love dictated the Rule, and though at times seemingly strict and severe, its purpose always is to serve the interests of love, to protect and strengthen it and make possible a more generous and more spontaneous response to the everlasting love of God. "The third degree of humility is that a person *for love of God* submit himself to his Superior in all obedience" (R 7).

In the Rule, St. Benedict always reserves the Latin word *amor* (love) for the love the disciple gives to God; *caritas* (charity) he uses for love directed to one's neighbor.

Love is the goal of the ascetical life, but also and most basically its prime mover, its source and principle. Quite often St. Benedict takes occasion to speak of the fear of God's judgments, of the desire to avoid hell. But he does it precisely because hell is the everlasting loss of that love relationship with God. When he addresses himself to the sometimes overwhelming difficulties of obedience, to the case of the brother upon whom "impossible things" have been laid, he appeals to the motive supreme, to love: "If after these representations the Superior still persists in his decision and command, let the subject know that this is for his good, and let him *obey out of love*, trusting in the help of God" (R 68).

In order to overcome obstacles we must turn for support to the love that God has for us and thereby bestir our love of him. Love is certainly the keystone of the whole spiritual edifice. Its power masters all difficulties, and helps the soul to conquer resistances and obstacles. Then, as the disciple goes from success to success, progress becomes easier and love more rewarding: "As we advance in the religious life and in faith, our hearts expand and we run the way of God's commandments with unspeakable sweetness of love" (R Prol). Nothing, however, matches St. Benedict's tribute to love at the end of the chapter on humility: "Having climbed all these steps of humility, therefore, the monk will presently come to that perfect love of God which casts out fear. And all those precepts which formerly he had not observed without fear he will now begin to keep by reason of that love, without any effort, as though naturally and by habit. No longer will his motive be the fear of hell, but rather the love of Christ, good habit and delight in the virtues which the Lord will deign to show forth by the Holy Spirit in his servant now cleansed from vice and sin" (R 7).

The disciple becomes love's possession, a person entirely under the direction of the Holy Spirit, receptive to the Spirit's least inspiration and in all things acting by that influence.

Never to Despair of God's Mercy

There is, sadly, the possibility of failure, of a life, if not completely ruined, at least disfigured by weaknesses and worse faults that expose the monk as a "liar before God by his tonsure" (R 1). Yet this is not sufficient reason to lose all hope and trust in the divine love. St. Benedict stresses the point in the final item on his long list detailing the instruments of good works. Never, he declares, are we justified in "despairing of God's mercy" (R 4).

If Christ preached the blessedness of the merciful, it was because the heart of God itself is infinitely merciful. So long as God's heart has compassion on the sinner who calls upon him, all is safe and God's love remains victorious. Everything that the history of salvation teaches us about God sings of his mercy in a canticle of creation and re-creation. In the final count, this is what we know about him, that he is merciful. Christ taught us that God's mercy is as boundless as his being and therefore is the fullness of mercy. This certitude of faith applies to our individual selves. What the history of salvation tells about God holds good for each one of us. Our personal history, with its rounds of faithfulness, of transgression, of return and repentance, is not much different from the history of God's people; it is the history of this people in miniature.

Despair impugns the basic character of God; it is an insult to the attribute that touches his heart most deeply; it as much as denies his love for the individual, the only case that matters, since there are only individuals (humanity being a collective entity, and impersonal). Consequently, St. Benedict forbids his followers ever to doubt God. The blood of God's Son is copious enough, the sources of grace abundant enough to trust in God in spite of all.

The final instrument of good works can redeem all the others. It is the last link in a golden chain that begins with the twofold commandment of love and binds the disciple to inviolable faith and trust in the divine love. Whatever wretchedness we may find in ourselves, we must hold fast to this love whose name, face to face with wretchedness, is mercy.

5

The Presence of God

At the end of the Prologue, St. Benedict remarks that it is with the same step that we, his disciples, progress in faith and in *conversatio* (i.e., the monastic life well lived). Our faith must grow day by day until we meet God. It is a divine largesse that must not lie idle but become fruitful. Vibrant, active faith carries us onward, from one improvement to another. Our life is a life of faith; it is steeped in faith, and continually confronts us with the invisible. The love disclosed to us and to which we pledge ourselves is a reality of faith, an object of faith, not a sensible experience. The God we seek is still a hidden God.

St. Benedict wants strong disciples like himself, persons resolved to serve with "loins girded with faith and the performance of good works" (R Prol; see Eph 6:14). Their faith is to be alive and operative, not a mere abstract perception with no effect on daily life but a conviction of the mind that translates into practice and is apparent in all external activities. Otherwise it is empty and in vain.

Faith presumes a choice. It pledges the whole being of the candidates to the monastic life. They enter upon this life seeking growth in the love of God. They give their faith and themselves to this love.

In faith there is a preliminary attraction, an aspiration that already is a gift. But faith needs to be fed so that the gift can remain strong and intact, and the soul retain its fervor.

God Present

At Vicovaro, St. Benedict tried for some months (or years) to govern a community of monks where everyone seemed bent on doing his own will. Faced with the hostility of these monks without ideal, who even tried to poison him, Benedict gave up: "May almighty God have mercy on you, brethren," he said in parting. "Why did you conspire to do this? Did I not tell you at the outset that my way of life would never harmonize with yours? Go and find yourselves an abbot to your liking. It is impossible for me to stay here any longer." With that, as St. Gregory notes, "he went back to the wilderness he loved, to live alone with himself *in the presence* of his heavenly Father" (D 3).

Benedict's life is not so much Benedict being present to God as God being present to him. The immensity of this objective presence filled his inner world. Before our gaze upon God there is God's gaze upon us, and St. Benedict had a deep sense of God being there, present and gazing upon him: the living and seeing God.

He believed in God's transcendence, in his infinite greatness and splendor that did not make him distant and unapproachable, shielded from the corruptions of the world and from things that pass. Benedict shunned both Gnosticism and Manicheism under any guise. God, he believed, would be less great were he not present with every form of being. As for problems raised by philosophers, the Abbot of Monte Cassino was not occupied with them. The God he knew and loved was the God of the Bible, the Most High, who at the same time is very near, solicitous of his children and waiting daily for their response to his love.

To a question asked by Gregory's foil, the deacon Peter, the Pope replied, "Blessed Benedict can be said to have lived 'with himself' because at all times he kept such close watch over his life and actions. By searching continually into his own soul he always beheld himself in the presence of his Creator. And this kept his mind from straying off to the world outside" (D 3). God's gazing presence led the saint to custody of the heart.

Here, without a doubt, the Dialogues touch on the Benedict of history. God's presence was a thought too much with him for Gregory's description to have been simply anecdotal. St. Benedict affirms the divine presence at every turn. God sees all; his gaze is fastened on us. The Abbot of Monte Cassino comes back to this again and again, repeating himself without scruple. It provides him with two major instruments of good works: "To keep constant guard over the actions of one's life," and "To know for certain that God sees one everywhere" (R 4). Everywhere, that is, and all the time; and to be convinced of it with a conviction that produces constant vigilance.

God is present in the soul; he sees it from within. All is transparent to him; there are no recesses that his gaze does not penetrate. He is present as onlooker; St. Benedict does not say as policeman. This onlooker is father, with a sort of anxiousness for the least signs of love, like a human father hovering over the cradle for just the hint of recognition from his infant child. God sees the inmost thoughts and desires, even those we shrink from admitting to ourselves. What is unperceived by others he sees from the inside, in its source. That is why, in principle, it should not be difficult to confess ourselves sinners before him.

God's presence is a basic truth, essential to the life of every Christian but especially to the person who comes to the community to cultivate watchfulness of the heart. St. Benedict inculcates the importance he attaches to God's presence. He makes it a principal consideration in his extensive treatment of humility, which (like the counterpart in the Rule of the Master) embodies the essential spirituality of the ancient fathers:

"Let us consider that God is always looking at us from heaven, that our actions are everywhere visible to the divine eyes. . . . This is what the prophet teaches us when he represents God as ever present within our thoughts, in the words, 'Searcher of minds and hearts is God' (Ps 7:9) and again in the words 'The Lord knows the thoughts of men' (Ps 94:11). Again he says, 'You have read my thoughts from afar' (Ps 139:2) and 'The thoughts of men will confess to you'" (Ps 75:11, Vulgate; R 7).

Not to be overlooked is that when introducing these scriptural voices in support of his own, St. Benedict first calls attention to the universality of the divine presence: "continually . . . always . . . everywhere." Absolutely nothing is excepted.

Benedict, never disdainful of repetition, expresses the same truth in the chapter on the manner of saying the Divine Office: "We believe that the divine presence is everywhere and that 'the eyes of the Lord are looking on the good and the evil in every place' (Prov 15:3). But we should believe this especially without any doubt when

we are assisting at the Work of God" (R 19). There is never a difference on God's part — his presence is always total. What varies is the
degree of attention to that presence and our being convinced of it,
which may be greater in one than another, or at one time than
another.

According to Gregory, St. Benedict shared in a limited way in
God's manner of being present. The Lord favored him with this
charismatic gift for the spiritual formation of his community, who
were largely monks in the rough, and particularly for making them
more heedful of the divine presence that never left them. If the man
of God could know their most secret thoughts and deeds, all the
more did the Lord know and see them. It was a training of their con-
science, and they learned with what care they must watch over it.

Sections 12–21 of Book II of the Dialogues feature this gift of
Benedict's. His spiritual presence to his disciples partook of God's
way of being present, though with limits. Some brethren had been
sent on an errand and, despite the prohibition of the Rule, had accepted a meal away from the monastery. They tried to conceal the
fact, but St. Benedict recounted it to them, what they ate and drank
and where. They confessed and asked forgiveness: "The man of God
did not hesitate to pardon them, confident that they would not do
further wrong in his absence, since they now realized he was always
present with them in spirit" (D 12). Another case in point is the
brother of the monk Valentinian. Contrary to his custom he had
broken his fast on the way to the monastery. Reproved for the irreg-
ularity, "he fell at Benedict's feet and admitted the weakness of his
will. The thought that even from such a distance the saint had wit-
nessed the wrong he had done filled him with shame and remorse"
(D 13).

Benedict's clairvoyance is shown on other occasions: the concealed flask of wine (D 18), the hidden handkerchiefs (D 19), the
thoughts of pride in a young monk (D 20): "At this the brethren all
realized that nothing could be kept secret from their holy abbot,
since he could hear even the unspoken sentiments of the heart." St.
Gregory attributes this gift for seeing the unseen to Benedict's constant adherence to the Lord, to his union with him: "The man who
unites himself to the Lord becomes one spirit with him" (1 Cor 6:17;
D 16).

Attention to the Presence

For Benedict, then, it is essential always to live under the eyes of God, to be conscious of his presence, our gaze meeting his, and our fervent but ever precarious attention responding to his, immutable as himself. God's presence commands custody of the heart: "So therefore, since the eyes of the Lord observe the good and the evil and the Lord is always looking down from heaven on the children of men 'to see if there be anyone who understands and seeks God,' . . . we must constantly beware, brethren, as the prophet says in the psalm, lest at any time God see us falling into evil ways and becoming unprofitable (Ps 53:2)" (R 7).

St. Benedict asks us, his followers, to accept the logic of our belief in God's objective presence, a belief that is first a truth and conviction of the mind but must not rest there. If God is always present, his presence should govern our conduct. Belief in God's abiding presence is fundamental to the spiritual life, since it begets attention to God as fruit of his attention to us, and becomes in consequence a steering principle of life, the rudder of moral conduct. Realizing that we are always in God's presence, we strive after truthfulness and reject deceit and hypocrisy. That others see or notice us becomes very secondary. But the more God's gazing presence impregnates our consciousness, the more we become what God wants of us.

The more, also, do we keep our eyes on God's standard of judgment. This judgment is not based on a kind of undercover surveillance and harassment. It is God's open, moral evaluation of our thoughts, words, deeds, desires. How we stand before God, this is what matters; or rather, nothing matters except this. If we keep his presence and standard of judgment constantly in mind, we soon discover in our lives what is of value in his sight and what is not. Trivialities, frivolities, things useless and vain, all are seen for what they are and handled accordingly. God's presence helps us conform to his will and is a constant reminder to practice custody of the heart. This is not a cult of the ego but a habitual self-examination with a view to controlling at the source the thoughts and desires of the heart; it is the soul looking more to God than to itself in an effort to gain greater likeness to him and become what he wants it to become.

In the language of the Bible and of St. Benedict, this respectful attention to God is called *the fear of the Lord*. Benedict makes it the moral foundation of the interior life. Fear of the Lord engenders humility. Love of God, humility, and fear of the Lord are the three poles around which St. Benedict's spiritual doctrine revolves. The three poles more or less converge in a single attitude comprising

piety, willing dependence, and respectful love. There is no disposi-
tion of the soul that he insists on more, as many chapters attest.

"The abbot should do all things in the fear of God" (R 3). The
disciple is to obey with such promptness and generosity that "at the
same moment the master's command is given and the disciple's work
is completed, the two things being speedily accomplished in the
swiftness of the fear of God . . ." (R 5). "The first degree of humility, then, is that a person keep the fear of God before his eyes and
beware of ever forgetting it" (R 7). In the cellarer[1] St. Benedict sees
almost a second in command, one who serves the abbot as temporal
administrator of the monastery; he is chosen from among "God-
fearing" monks (R 31). The infirmarian is to be an "attendant who is
God-fearing" (R 36). The guesthouse should be in charge of "a
brother whose soul is possessed by the fear of God" (R 53). Choice of
a Prior, if circumstances require one, should be made by the abbot
"with counsel of God-fearing brethren" (R 65). Election of an abbot
is to be conducted "in the fear of God" (R 64). Fear of the Lord will
inspire the porter to be prompt in attending to guests and the poor,
with the warmth of charity (R 66). Finally, in the chapter on good
zeal St. Benedict has this splendid phrase, probably taken from St.
Ambrose: "to fear God in love" (R 72).

Living under God's presence, the disciples feel both very small
and very loved, and aim respectfully to return love for love. We are
careful not to prove unworthy of the Lord who condescends to cast
eyes on us. We seek after God, who alone counts, with an attitude of
humility and love. In short, we practice what St. Benedict calls
perfection.

Seeing with the Eyes of God

As we truly live in the presence of God we come to the point
where God's standard of judgment is also ours. Things have value
for us only if they have value for God. It is a case of the primacy of
the spiritual being absolute, and faith the measure of all things.
Around us we in a sense see only God. We are truly in the service of
the Lord, as we resolved upon entering the community. Our whole
lives are God-centered and lived in an atmosphere of praise: "That
in all things God may be glorified" (R 57). Menial tasks are reli-

---

[1] The monk in charge of the storeroom (warehouse), responsible for monastic
property and from whom community members received what they were authorized to
have. "Procurator" or "corporation treasurer" are the terms more commonly used
nowadays.

giously performed and the least goods and chattels of the monastery treated with scrupulous care: "Let him regard all the utensils of the monastery and its whole property as if they were the sacred vessels of the altar" (R 31).

God not only is present; he presides over the community life. St. Benedict wants the community to take note of this and to recognize it wherever or through whomever it is manifested. In this spirit he prescribes that the younger members should not be excluded when the brethren are called to counsel: "The Lord often reveals to the younger what is best" (R 3). Moreover, the abbot will listen to the advice or suggestions of a pilgrim monk: "If this monk censures or points out anything reasonably and with the humility of charity, let the abbot consider prudently whether perhaps it was for that very purpose that the Lord sent him" (R 61).

Nothing is more characteristic of the Rule than its continual appeal to the light of faith, its demand to go beyond appearances to the solid reality of God's norm and judgment. This gives monastic life a firm stability and a gravity of purpose throughout. It allows every task to be taken in earnest and performed with humility and in a manner to edify, as St. Benedict requires of the singing or reading of the psalms at the Work of God (R 47).

If we are determined that God's point of view prevails in our lives, we are not surprised when the inevitable trials overtake us. No love compares with the love of the heavenly Father. Yet it was his love that designed the Cross for his only Son. To those who belong to his Son, the same love means a measure of participation in his redemptive suffering. Candidates for the monastic life are not to be received without testing their capacity for living by these truths of faith. It is important to determine "whether he bears patiently the harsh treatment offered him." The senior charged with the novice's initiation shall carefully examine if "the novice is truly seeking God, and whether he is zealous for the Work of God, for obedience and for humiliations. Let the novice be told all the hard and rugged ways by which the journey to God is made" (R 58).

During one's monastic career there will be many a time when the disciple's faith is put to the test and must prove itself: times when a person might give way to discouragement, times when he or she receives what seems to be inequitable treatment, and any number of similar situations. St. Benedict anticipates these periods in a disciple's life and offers a recipe: "The fourth degree of humility is that he hold fast to patience with a silent mind when in this obedience he meets with difficulties and contradictions and even any kind of injustice, enduring all without wearying or running away. . . . To show how those who are faithful ought to endure all things, however contrary, for the Lord, the Scripture says in the person of the sufferers: 'For your sake we are put to death all the day long; we are considered as sheep marked for slaughter (Ps 44:22)'" (R 7).

In these circumstances we not only remember God's sense of value but bravely espouse it. We adopt the divine way of seeing things and do what is right to the Lord although it seems foolishness to others: "By their patience those faithful ones fulfil the Lord's command in adversities and injuries: when struck on one cheek, they offer the other; when deprived of their tunic, they surrender also their cloak; when forced to go a mile, they go two (see Matt 5:39-41)" (R 7).

The disciples who have arrived at this perfect conformity with God's will and intention are never closer to him than at such times of sore distress. It is then that we truly "by patience share in the sufferings of Christ" (R Prol). The victory we gain may be known only to God, whose invisible presence is with us, uplifting and all-powerful, as once it was with the martyrs.

6

Chᴿιst

Gregory makes Benedict a contemplative. He shows him toward the end of his life in a mystical vision in which the world appeared to him both transfigured and reduced to its proper proportions. St. Gregory elucidates: "The light of holy contemplation enlarges and expands the mind. . . . The soul that sees God rises even above itself, and as it is drawn upward in his light all its inner powers unfold. Then, when it looks down from above, it sees how small everything really is that was beyond its grasp before" (D 35). But curiously, the biographer makes little mention of Christ. Yet Benedict was devoted to the God-man; his name is virtually on every page of the Rule, and the disciple looks constantly to him.

Much closer on this point to the spirit of their lawgiver were the monks of Cluny, who depicted a majestic Christ in the apse of their churches. From high above he dominated their liturgical life; all eyes were on him, all hearts and minds converged in him. The majestic Christ of the basilica built by St. Hugo disappeared with the ruins of the abbey church, but something of what must have been its admirable composition can be gathered from a painting at the present-day priory of Berzé-la-Ville:[1] Christ in glory, in regal robes

---

[1] Near Sologyn, canton of Mâcon (Saône-et-Loire).

43

and purple mantle, the full figure borne aloft against the azure fir-
mament that in former times would have been studded with gold
and silver stars—a magnificent painting, drawn with a master's
touch that captures the spirit of Byzantine mosaics.

For St. Benedict, Christ is the *Pantocrator*, the Lord All-
powerful. Living in an Italy dominated by Arians, he reacted with
all the strength of his faith against the heresy of the invaders and
asserted the full divinity of Christ the King, "the true King," he says
with emphasis (R Prol).

From the very beginning of the Rule he brings forward for the
candidate's allegiance the Christ of sovereign majesty: "To you,
therefore, my words are now addressed, whoever you may be, who
are renouncing your own will to do battle under the Lord Christ,
the true King, and are taking up the strong, bright weapons of obedience" (R Prol).

The Word Incarnate

Benedict's preferred title for Christ is Lord, a name of God
which he also uses for the Trinity acting as one. Christ is the Lord
who is served, the King under whom battle is done (R 61). All his
followers "bear an equal burden of service in the army of the same
Lord" (R 2).

Benedict insists on the divinity of Christ. He is God and therefore his presence is the presence of God; it encompasses the present,
the past, and the future. The disciple is in contact with him;
dialogue is possible as between two living persons. Christ does not
belong only to history; he is present now and everywhere. His voice
is the voice of God. It is he who is petitioned for the grace to overcome obstacles, he to whom the abbot must render an account. His
presence reaches into every corner of monastic life, whose goal is
none other than to draw the monk into closest communion with
him.

Since Christ is Lord, the disciple becomes his servant in a service of love. The notion of service is extremely important in the Rule.
It is made the correlative of *militare*, to fight, to do battle. Sulpicius
Severus, biographer of the bishop St. Martin of Tours, described
him as *servus Dei, servus Christi*, servant of God, servant of Christ.
The spirit of the saintly bishop, the spirit of service and combat,
breathes in St. Benedict, who held him in veneration and dedicated
to him one of the oratories at Cassino.

Because of the scope of Christ's lordship, before whom all knees bend on earth, in heaven, and under the earth, our service is total and all-inclusive. Our belonging to Christ means a radical conversion, with absolute dispossession of oneself. We make a total renunciation that leaves nothing of ourselves as our own. We voluntarily enter upon a condition of complete dependence: "The novice knows that from that day forward he will no longer have power even over his own body" (R 58); "they are not permitted to have even their bodies or wills at their own disposal" (R 33).

Another name St. Benedict uses for Christ is King. The title harks back to the Greek *Basileus*, the designation of Byzantine emperors whose dominion in principle extended to the whole Roman Empire of antiquity, East and West, and whose prestige was immense. The tile is not found in the Rule of the Master. But if Christ is King, the disciple is his soldier. The vocabulary of combat is traditional in monachism. The hermits, says St. Benedict, are those "who, no longer in the first fervor of their reformation, but after long probation in a monastery, having learned by the help of many brethren how to fight against the devil, go out well armed from the ranks of the community to the solitary combat of the desert. They are able now, with no help save from God, to fight single-handed against the vices of the flesh and their own evil thoughts" (R 1). Cenobites also are in combat, but as part of an army, "serving under a rule and an abbot" (*Ibid.*).

Because of their service to their divine leader, the disciples have every confidence of one day meriting "to see him who has called us to his kingdom" (R Prol).

In regard to the humanity of Christ, Benedict is reserved; he does not wear his devotion on his sleeve. He knows the gospels well, urges them upon the disciple, and quotes them profusely. He conceives of monastic life as participation in the sufferings of Christ, but does not give the Lord his personal name, Jesus. The tenderness of his love for the Lord is left more or less unspoken. Instead, he prefers to show it in the warmth and care he wants bestowed on Christ's little ones, the lowly and the poor. There his love for the God-man is far from being reserved.

The Earthly Image of Christ: the Abbot

Christ came to teach his disciples, and through them the world. St. Benedict puts his followers in contact with God's word that is essentially the word and message of Christ. In the hearing of the Word, in *lectio divina*, in prayer, the disciples hear Christ speaking.

But in addition, the author of the Rule has entrusted the abbot himself with a teaching mission to his disciples. He is steward of God's word. He is spokesman of Christ, in two ways: by his teaching based on the gospel, and by his example: "He ought to govern his disciples with a twofold teaching. That is to say, he should show them all that is good and holy by his deeds even more than by his words, expounding the Lord's commandments in words to the intelligent among his disciples, but demonstrating the divine precepts by his actions for those of harder hearts and ruder minds" (R 2).

Perhaps St. Benedict thought the title "master" too human to be applied to Christ. He limits it to helpers and stand-ins: specifically himself and all abbots. The master who speaks in the Prologue of the Rule is indeed St. Benedict, but he realizes that one day he must leave the world and someone else will have to administer the Rule. In the structure of community life the abbot is the cornerstone; the whole edifice rests on him. Benedict sees in him a sort of Rule in the flesh. And as father he is in some way the soul of the community: "[The abbot] is believed to hold the place of Christ in the monastery, being called by a name of his, which is taken from the words of the apostle: 'You have received a spirit of the adoption as sons by virtue of which we cry "Abba, Father!"'" (R 2; see Rom 8:15).

Consequently, it is the abbot who has the ultimate responsibility in forming the disciples of Christ who are in the school of the Lord's service, the place of apprenticeship where they are in training for service to their King.

The abbot is the sacrament of Christ. If there is one divine attribute that outshines all others in the life of our Lord, it is the quality of mercy. Hence the abbot likewise should be imbued with mercy for the betterment of the souls entrusted to him. St. Benedict cautions him against a sort of pseudo-efficiency, namely, overinvolvement in the temporalities of the monastery to the detriment of the spiritual: "Above all let him not neglect or undervalue the welfare of the souls committed to him, in a greater concern for fleeting, earthly, perishable things; but let him always bear in mind that he has undertaken the government of souls and that he will have to give an account of them" (R 2).

But even in the realm of the spiritual, the realm of the Lord's service proper, the abbot must guard against another kind of pseudo-efficiency, namely, the imbalance of stinting the attention he gives to some while spending more time on others simply because they are more amenable to his tutelage, perform their tasks more generously, and are making greater progress in the way of the Lord. St. Benedict makes it a duty of the abbot to imitate the care and concern of the Good Shepherd by preferring the sick, the infirm, and the weak, and above all by seeking after the strayed and the lost. He is to be father, like Christ.

Christ-Father

If Benedict wants the abbot to be father, it is because he has an exalted view of the fatherhood he finds in Christ. The abbot is the vicar of Christ-Father for all his disciples. He is Christ's envoy to each of them, sent to represent him. But the abbot is only a lieutenant, i.e., acting in the place and in the name of Christ. The family he governs is not his, but Christ's. The teaching he imparts is not his, it is Christ's. The disciples upon whom he bestows his care are not his; they are children of God, such as Christ called "my little children."

Father is one who begets, who gives life. The sapiential books of the Bible abound in the vocabulary of fatherhood, for there is a real fatherhood of the spiritual order. St. Benedict knew it well, learning it from the whole monastic tradition. Like the Rule of the Master, he perceived the doctrinal fatherhood exercised by Christ, whose relations with his disciples often assumed this character. Our Lord did not want to leave his own "orphans." He compared himself to the hen gathering the young under her wings. He called his disciples "my little children" or "children," as did the doctors of wisdom in Israel.

In the Rule of the Master, Christ is considered "Father," and the Lord's Prayer is even addressed to him: "Our Father, who art in heaven." He is also considered Lord, Creator, source of all grace, head of the new race. St. Benedict is less inclined than the Master to give Christ the name of Father. But in chapter 2 he does speak of him as Father of the family and master of the house of which the abbot is steward: "Let the abbot be sure that any lack of profit the master of the house may find in the sheep will be laid to the blame of the shepherd" (R 2).

In the Prologue, Benedict introduces himself as master and requests his readers to listen as he calls them to serve Jesus Christ, true King. Christ continues to be the focus as the Prologue unfolds. He it is who is beseeched to strengthen the monastic will and purpose, who deigns to count the disciple among his children, but who also is the angered Father and stern master delivering to eternal punishment the wicked servants.

Unless, therefore, one is prepared to deny all coherence to St. Benedict's thought and its development in the Rule, the only possible conclusion is that for him Christ is Father and that the disciple is joined to Christ as to Father, by ties of kinship.

In the body of the Rule the Lord appears as shepherd and owner of the flock. Shepherd emphasizes his care for the sheep, the community (R 27). Owner indicates that the abbot is simply the Lord's shepherd, charged by him with pasturing the flock (R 1, 2, 27). The abbot, then, is shepherd, but by derivative and subordinate title. There is only one shepherd: Christ. The abbot has custody of the flock, but it is delegated custody. The sheep are "entrusted" to him, and the flock is left for him to watch under the vigilance of the "Pius Pastor," invisibly yet truly present.

Complementing Christ's image as shepherd is the image of physician. Christ is physician. So is the abbot, but again dependently. St. Benedict has any number of words and expressions relating to the abbot's curative role: every remedy, unhealthy behavior (R 2); the healthy, the sick, wise physician (R 27); applications, the ointments of exhortation, the medicines of the holy Scriptures, the cautery of excommunication, the knife of amputation, contaminate, restore health (R 28). But only Christ can heal, and the most efficacious remedy is prayer, "so that the Lord, who can do all things, may restore health to the sick brother" (R 28). Recourse to Christ is the ultimate remedy.

Following and Imitating Christ

The disciple enlists in the service of Christ the King. His kingdom, the Kingdom of God, dominates the monastic ideal. The faith by which the disciples bind themselves to the Lord involves all aspects of their lives; they turn from themselves to follow someone else.

Flight from the world is a common theme of the spiritual life. Was it the theme Gregory the Great wanted to illustrate in the case of St. Benedict at the beginning of Dialogues II? One cannot be certain. The boy Benedict had the courage of an elder. He judges as though from long experience. He seems to have skipped adolescence and sizes things according to their true value. In the rose offered him he sees the wilted flower. He abandons the world, not waiting for the world to abandon him. He disdains; he leaves, dons the habit — pledge of a religious life — and pursues his desire "to please God alone."

Gregory, moreover, does not mention the idea of seeking Christ, but Benedict himself refers to it constantly: "To deny oneself in order to follow Christ," he remarks in the instruments of good works (R 4). But renunciation is not an end in itself. Abandonment of self is for the purpose of belonging to another. We follow Christ, we follow the Rule, or, by a disastrous turning back that is the contrary of conversion, we follow our own will. We have a choice. Following Christ is not possible without self-renunciation. The basic error of false disciples (the vagabonds and those without a superior) is to believe that monastic life is possible without actual obedience: "Their law is the desire for self-gratification: whatever enters their mind or appeals to them, that they call holy; what they dislike, they regard as unlawful" (R 1).

The true disciple lives under obedience, and through it gives concrete expression to the following of Christ. That obedience is prompt, earnest, buoyant and cheerful, with fidelity to the command given: "Obedience without delay is the virtue of those who hold nothing dearer to them than Christ; who, because of the holy service they have professed, and the fear of hell, and the glory of life everlasting, as soon as anything has been ordered by the superior, receive it as a divine command and cannot suffer any delay in executing it" (R 5).

True obedience is fervent, energetic, even enthusiastic, and implies perfect docility. The disciple's aim and ambition should be nothing less than to attain this docility so that one is counted among those who "are living up to that maxim of the Lord in which he says, 'I have come not to do my own will, but the will of him who sent me'" (R 5; see John 6:38). What is wanted is obedience and good will combined, given to superiors, of course, but ultimately to God (R 5).

St. Benedict values holy obedience as the most perfect imitation of Christ. He speaks to this effect in the second and third degree of humility: "The second degree of humility is that a person love not his own will nor take pleasure in satisfying his own desires, but model his actions on the saying of the Lord, 'I have come not to do my own will, but the will of him who sent me' (John 6:38)." This makes the second time that he uses this verse of St. John. "The third degree of humility is that a person for love of God submit himself to his superior in all obedience, imitating the Lord, of whom the apostle says, 'He became obedient even unto death'" (R 7; see Phil 2:8).

The disorder caused by sin is essentially repaired in baptism, but full restoration of the soul's health and vitality takes time. The days of this life are granted for this purpose, days of reprieve to perfect the Christ life in us. Obedience, which implies complete renunciation of whatever is cause or occasion of sin, is the most assured means to this end. Conformity of will is the fruit of love, and its proof.

For love of Christ the disciples strive to carry out the will of another and to sacrifice their own inclinations. They forget themselves in order to become all things to all, which is the key to repaying Christ's love in every circumstance. "Not only is the boon of obedience to be shown by all to the abbot, but the brethren are also to obey one another, knowing that by this road of obedience they are going to God" (R 71). St. Cyprian, whom St. Benedict quotes indirectly a number of times, says, "Since Christ places nothing above our interests, let us not place anything above Christ."[2]

Christ's example inspires the disciples to love their persecutors: "To pray for one's enemies in the love of Christ" (R 4). When the Lord was despised, humiliated, rejected, and crucified, he loved those who made him suffer. He was brutalized, made a common criminal, tyrannized, and tormented. He could not but feel keenly the opprobrium and degradation heaped upon him, if only extrinsic; his human dignity rebelled against it. In these circumstances, especially in these circumstances, Christ continued to love. He requires the same of his disciples. He does not promise them rank and adulation, only scorn, humiliation, and crucifixion, his own portion on earth. It is not enough to love Christ who sends this sometimes overwhelming suffering; we have also to love those who inflict it, deserved or not.

Imitation of Christ places the disciples at the heart of his mystery; it gives them experiential knowledge of the economy of redemption, which is salvation through the Cross. At the center of human history stands the Easter mystery, life gained through death. This will always be incomprehensible to minds not enlightened by faith. Christ became obedient unto death, to death on a cross. In fulfillment of the Father's will he gave his life as an offering of love and an act of supreme adoration. Monastic life gives the Christian the means of achieving a similar obedience. By becoming disciples we join the imitators of Christ. Through an act of renunciation that

---

[2] St. Cyprian, *De oratione dominica*, c. 15, *PL*, IV, 520.

has continually to be renewed, we strike at the root of all disobedience and rebellion: our own wills. We lose life to gain it; we experience the paradox that life is saved in losing it.

St. Benedict asks his followers to die to themselves, to become willing participants through the monastic life in the sufferings of Christ (R Prol). To this end we must abandon ourselves through a radical abnegation that is similar to dying. But this work of death, like the death of Christ on the cross, is inseparably a work of life. The Easter mystery interprets this process and gives it its meaning. There are bonds to break, a servitude to get free from at the cost of sacrifice and renunciation. The passion of Christ is the model that the disciples keep before them: "Never departing from his school, but persevering in the monastery according to his teaching until death, we may by patience share in the sufferings of Christ and deserve to have a share also in his kingdom" (R Prol).

The disciple looks forward to the eternal Easter, to meeting the risen Christ with the joy the Spirit gives and with the desire the Spirit arouses. Like St. Ignatius of Antioch we can say: "Him I seek, the Jesus who died for us; him I want, the Jesus who rose for us. Let me have my wish, let me imitate the passion of my God."[3]

To Prefer Nothing to the Love of Christ

This is a thought dear to St. Benedict, and the formula itself is a favorite of his, repeated three times: in essence in the chapter on obedience (R 5), and literally in the chapter on the instruments of good works (R 4) and the chapter on good zeal (R 72). He did not invent it. He read it in St. Cyprian's explanation of the Our Father, in St. Athanasius' life of St. Anthony, father of monks, in St. Augustine's commentaries on the psalms, Psalm 29 in particular.

St. Benedict wants our love to be exclusive, a sovereign and dominant love that merges our wills with the will of the Lord. The ideal is Christ's love for the Father. When there is a conflict of love, we do not barter; the love of Christ prevails. The Son of God came to dwell among us. We come to understand this with the literalness of simple folk. We do all in our power to make our hearts Christ's abode. Our lives are not governed in the first instance by an abstract moral law, though we know and are devoted to this law and appreciate its value. But what governs our lives most truly is the person who has won our hearts.

[3] Ignatius of Antioch, *Letter to the Romans*, c. 6.

Christ is our one treasure, our one love. Having Christ, our abnegation becomes easier, our temptations less threatening, since we have only to call upon him in every need. To earn the beautiful title of disciple we are prepared to renounce every other good, beginning with ourselves. We frown on false riches that might swell our pride or otherwise encumber us. We go so far as to live as strangers to the world, if only we gain the love of Christ. Christ is Benedict's whole life.

Christ in Human Faces

The Abbot of Cassino urges his disciples to develop a working faith, one that recognizes Christ in whomever he appears. It can be said without exaggeration that for faith that is alive and alert there is only Christ. The disciple sees him everywhere. In the abbot, first of all, whose place he holds in the monastery and therefore is given a name which strictly befits only Christ: "The abbot, since he is believed to represent Christ, shall be called Lord and Abbot, not for any pretensions of his own but out of honor and love for Christ" (R 63). In the guests of the monastery: "Let all guests who arrive be received like Christ, for he is going to say: 'I came as a guest, and you received me' (Matt 25:35)" (R 53). In the poor, in travelers and strangers, people one knows not whence they came, "because it is especially in them that Christ is received" (Ibid.). In the sick: "Before all things and above all things, care must be taken of the sick, so that they will be served as if they were Christ in person; for he himself said, 'I was sick, and you visited me' (Matt 25:36) and, 'What you did for one of these least ones, you did for me' (Matt 25:40)" (R 36). Christ is also met in priests and indeed in all. Christ seen in all is the reason for the honor and deference paid to all: "Let the head be bowed or the whole body prostrated on the ground in adoration of Christ, who indeed is received in their person" (R 53).

Benedict's chapter on receiving guests is intriguing and deserves a closer look. The reception is warm, prompt, and respectful. It is motivated by the charity of Christ that inspires every attention. According to the ritual laid down in the Rule, it begins with prayer with the guests to thank God for this meeting and the grace he sends with the guests. Then the kiss of peace is exchanged, after which they are led to the oratory for a longer period of prayer and lectio divina, i.e., some portions of sacred reading. Reception in the refectory follows, where the abbot gives them water for their hands. In addition and at an opportune moment, both abbot and community wash the guests' feet.

This ritual has been compared, with a difference, to what happened when Simon the Pharisee received our Lord (Luke 7:36f.). Simon did not wash Christ's feet, did not welcome him with a kiss nor anoint his head with oil. The disciples now want to erase the memory of this negligence, this lack of feeling. They desire to compensate for the coolness of Simon's reception by imitating the fervor of the sinful woman. They know they also are sinners and by proving their love in this way hope to obtain the forgiveness she received because she loved much. Their hope is not confounded, and they testify to it in the psalm verse that concludes the *mandatum*[4] (washing of feet): *Suscepimus, Deus, misericordiam tuam,* "We have received your mercy, O Lord, in the midst of your temple" (Ps 48:10). The Lord's forgiveness, his mercy came with the guests they made welcome.

We therefore meet Christ everywhere. This is the joy of our lives and the reason we feel blessed in the community and there live the "good days" of the Prologue, in the house of God. We live in communion with Christ who called us, and living close to Christ, we are close to the community. Our hearts know only one love that is shed on every creature, because we see in all an image of the Christ we love.

As for the community itself, it becomes, as did the cave at Subiaco, "a light that warms the whole countryside with the love of God, our Lord and Savior Jesus Christ." It is a pole of attraction for numerous souls who come "to bring their heart under the light yoke of their Savior" (D 8).

---

[4] The "Commandment," the name of the first chant that accompanied the washing of feet. The allusion is to John 13:34: "A new commandment I give to you, that you love one another even as I have loved you."

7

GRACE

In St. Augustine, Benedict found a doctrine of monastic life that enabled him to correct certain exaggerations in his principal source, the Rule of the Master. At the same time, he had no difficulty in making use of an author like Cassian, whose position on the problem of grace differed significantly from Augustine. Benedict somehow was not troubled by this seeming inconsistency, and though generally sharp-eyed in regard to orthodoxy and the canonicity of the sacred books, he could make an unqualified recommendation of Cassian to his followers and even made him standard reading at Compline: "As soon as they have risen from supper they shall all sit together, and one of them shall read the Conferences of Cassian or the Lives of the Fathers or something else that may edify the hearers" (R 42).

Obviously, Benedict did not consider Cassian a dangerous author. From Cassiodorus, a contemporary of Benedict, we know that copies of Cassian, with his errors on grace expurgated by Bishop Victor, were soon in circulation, but there is nothing in the record to indicate that the Abbot of Cassino was acquainted with them. In all probability, then, it was an unwashed Cassian that he recommended. Actually, the author of the Conferences did not agree with the teachings of Pelagius, whom he disliked, but the Augustinian refutation seemed too extreme and therefore dangerous. Cassian's own views, for the most part, are expressed in Conference 13 and prevailed in French monachism until the Council of Orange in 529.

In that year Pope Felix IV sent a collection of small excerpts (*capitula*) to Caesarius of Arles, some of which were almost verbatim passages from St. Augustine's writings, others from Prosper of Aquitaine. About a dozen bishops of Narbonnaise Gaul who had come together for the dedication of a church at Orange received and subscribed to the excerpts sent by the Pope and, it seems, added some comments of their own. But neither the Council of Orange nor Caesarius of Arles, who presided, were prepared to take explicit action against Cassian. The author of the Conferences was not condemned by name till some time later, toward the middle of the sixth century in a false decretal issued under the name of Pope Gelasius.

When Benedict was writing his Rule the authority of Cassian had not yet been questioned. Some statements of the Rule could be interpreted in a semi-Pelagian sense while others are in agreement with the Augustinian position. St. Benedict does not speak as a theologian but as an ascetical writer whose purpose is to direct the moral effort of his disciples.

Nevertheless, the problem of grace did occupy his mind. He gives indications of it in more than fifteen passages, and corrects certain extremes in the Rule of the Master to make them more orthodox. Benedict understood the absolute necessity of grace, our utter need of it. He realized that the weakness and imperfection of fallen humanity calls for constant, urgent recourse to God in humble and fervent prayer. Every good, moral or other, is a reflection of God and comes from him.

The Action of Grace

The first reference to grace at the beginning of the Prologue might be seen as Pelagian in tone because apparently it leaves the first initiative of conversion to us. But it is clear that St. Benedict is speaking from the psychological level, the level of conscious experience, not of intrinsic or subconscious being: "And first of all, whatever good work you begin to do, beg of him [the Lord Jesus Christ] with most earnest prayer to perfect it" (R Prol).

Benedict wants the disciple to begin with prayer: prayer that signifies humility, fundamental helplessness, and a plea to God's infinite mercy. We must build on humility.

Humility is indispensable. Without it, there is no hope of reaching the eternal tents, the tabernacle of the kingdom. Those who shall enter there "fearing the Lord, do not pride themselves on their good observance; but, convinced that the good which is in them cannot come from themselves but must come from the Lord, glorify the Lord's work in them, using the words of the prophet, 'Not to us, O Lord, not to us, but to your name give the glory' (Ps 115:1). Thus also the apostle Paul attributed nothing of the success of his preaching to himself, but said, 'By the grace of God I am what I am' (1 Cor 15:10). And again he says, 'He who glories, let him glory in the Lord' (2 Cor 10:17)" (R Prol).

These words, inserted in the first pages of the Rule, are indicative of Benedict the Lawgiver's thought and cast their light on the entire code of the perfect life he envisions. A person acts, but under God's movement, and the whole journey to the goal is kept going through the care and watchfulness of Christ the Lord. The disciple strives at all times to obey by help of "the good things he has given us" (R Prol). These good things are among the Lord's first gifts; they are talents to be multiplied. Without them, nothing would be undertaken.

In time of difficulty, Benedict urges us to turn to prayer, while keeping our wits about us and not magnifying obstacles. With God's help, everything can be overcome or coped with: "Let us ask God that he be pleased to give us the help of his grace for anything which our nature finds hardly possible" (R Prol). Benedict's language, here as elsewhere, may not be theologically refined. He speaks more like the parables of our Lord, in simile and metaphor. He is a spiritual master using words and expressions most apt to be understood by his beginners in the monastic life, those who could be former slaves or barbarians like the humbled Goth of the Dialogues.

All through the Rule, usually in short formulas, St. Benedict directs attention to the role of grace so that no one might forget it in practice: "by means of God's help," "with the help of God," etc. In the instruments of good works he comes more to the point, and in two consecutive instruments sums up what he teaches in the Prologue concerning God's role in the disciple's sanctification: "To attribute to God, and not to self, whatever good one sees in oneself. But to recognize always that the evil is one's own doing, and to impute it to oneself" (R 4, 42–43). To each his due. Free will exists with the unhappy possibility of failure. But God is not responsible for the failures.

In the chapter on humility Benedict again stresses the work of grace, this time illustrating it with the symbolic ladder of Jacob: "The ladder thus set up is our life in the world, which the Lord raises up to heaven if our heart is humbled. For we call our body and soul the sides of the ladder, and into these sides our divine vocation has inserted the different steps of humility and discipline we must climb" (R 7). No doubt is possible here. Unlike Cassian in Conference 13, Benedict attributes to God the initiative in the first movement toward conversion: it is grace that calls, the grace of God. It is the Lord who gradually raises up the life of the disciple to reach the Lord, provided the disciple enters in earnest upon the way of humility. And it is grace that prepares the steps of humility one must climb, or rather which it enables one to climb.

Grace is there, invisible and invisibly working. It is up to us to conform to its attraction. Sometimes it gently prods us to prolong our prayer (R 20); sometimes there is special need to implore it for ourselves or others. Prayer is the last resort when all other supernatural means have failed, but it is supremely powerful. If a recalcitrant follower persists in errant behavior, the abbot need not despair: "Let him apply a still greater remedy, his own prayers and those of all the brethren, that the Lord, who can do all things, may restore health to the sick brother" (R 28).

God did not create human beings from the same mold. Each is a distinctive person. In the supernatural order there is a comparable distinction of gifts so that God's infinite riches might be manifested. Everyone has his or her own gift or grace to which to conform (R 40).

The disciples have confidence in God's grace, in its necessity and efficacy. With it, they feel equal to all challenges. The will of God has only to be clearly shown, to be communicated, and they know they can count on grace to meet the most formidable difficulties, the "impossible things" of Chapter 68. If the superior enjoins them in full knowledge of the case and stands on his or her command, the disciples go ahead "trusting in the help of God." In fact, is not the monastic life as such one of these "impossible" things? A person alone has not the strength for it. Nevertheless, the life can, indeed must be led with complete assurance. God is there with his grace to provide for every need so long as the disciple is engaged in what is clearly God's will and plan for that person.

The Rule ends on a note of confidence, of ultimate success in the monastic life: "You will attain. . . ." The disciple's hope is not idle, but it is not placed in what another person provides. Success will be due to "God's protection." In hope of attaining the contemplation that is to crown our quest of God, we set to work, our resolution supported by grace: "Fulfill with the help of Christ, this minimum Rule which we have written for beginners" (R 73).

The Necessity of Human Cooperation

St. Benedict is not a quietist. When treating of the steps of progress in the spiritual life, he does not overlook ascetical practice and combat. He points out the necessity of action for making headway. It is through positive acts that our lives give evidence of bearing fruit. God expects that "we respond by our deeds" (R Prol). The author of the Rule wants this response to be strong, vigorous, and unremitting. To this end he supplies his followers with the instruments of good works, tools they must constantly use day and night without relaxing (R 4). St. Benedict is a realist; he asks for deeds, not words. At the same time, he is careful not to exaggerate ascetical practice and glorify the human part. It is grace that conducts everything, from the first call to the monastic life to its final achievement.

Nevertheless, the Lord seeks doers, workers. Like the master of the vineyard, he goes to the marketplace to recruit them "in the multitude." To those who answer his call, he offers a program: "If you will have true and everlasting life, keep your tongue from evil and your lips that they speak no guile. Turn away from evil and do good; seek after peace and pursue it" (R Prol; see Ps 34:13-14).

God's grace is not a substitute for our activity. Grace evokes it, supports it, and makes it efficacious. Grace permits us to accomplish the works prescribed by God and to do so in a manner pleasing to God. It is a divine work that we perform, *opus Dei*. Traditionally, the "Work of God" refers to the whole life of the disciples who are workers at a task they cannot handle by themselves, whose dimensions are divine. Every work we are asked to perform is steeped in God.

It is not possible, in other words, to progress to God without the help and support of God. The work of sanctification is a co-operation, a joint work. The soul yields freely to the movements of grace and calls upon all its resources to quell resistance. The interior agent of its sanctification is the Spirit of God, and the attraction of love that it experiences as it progresses is a sign of the Spirit's presence.

By a kind of paradox, St. Benedict is very conscious of our

8

PRAYER

Benedict's disciples chant much, and the chant is joyous. Love of God, love of Christ account for the monastic life. God's free gift calls for the response of love, freely given like his. The disciple has freely received and freely returns in gladness. It is an inner joy, reflected in song and praise.

Adoration is a duty of the creature. The gospel did not abolish this duty but put it on a higher level by enhancing the relationship that unites creature and Creator. It became a filial relationship marked by freedom and spontaneity.

Religion seeks expression in love and cultic worship inspired by love. The followers of St. Benedict live in community and chant in community. The habitual joy that pervades their life is periodically refreshed in the celebration of Easter, in the celebration of Sunday, the weekly Easter, and the feasts of patron saints. Every celebration was for them a foretaste of the feast of eternity, the eternal Easter: "Love sings now," says St. Augustine, "and love will sing then; but now it is a famished love that sings, then it will be a sated love."[1]

Easter brightens the entire liturgical year, the "holy Easter" (St.

---

[1] St. Augustine, *Sermon 255*, n. 5, *PL* 38, 1183.

limitations, our weaknesses, and our unstable and dilatory nature. The author of the Rule wanted to "introduce nothing harsh or burdensome" (R Prol). He weighs the pros and cons; he stretches the measure of indulgence. Yet he is convinced that human limitations can be surmounted through the all-powerful action of grace, and he turns unceasingly to this hidden reserve (too often ignored or slighted) of spiritual energy. He does not commit his disciples to works that have no purpose other than an ascetical exercise, as though an end in itself, but leads them on toward a kind of spiritual self-transcendence; to this he sets no limits, trusting the omnipotence of God to produce marvels of grace.

Grace, then, is absolutely necessary not only to begin a meritorious action but also to sustain it and realize its full potential. Our spiritual effort is a response. God takes the initiative; he speaks, he calls; he touches the heart of the one he calls. We hear the voice inviting us and consent to obey. This obedience is a difficult work; it does not come without effort. We either cooperate with grace or we do not. We possess gifts given by God that we must bring to fruit. God puts at our disposal the instruments to be used. The most valuable of these is the prayer that confesses our helplessness and declares our reliance on God all-powerful. Watchfulness and personal effort are the rule.

Most assuredly, it is with Christ's help and with his grace that any true virtue takes root in the soul. Yet these terms—God's help, God's assistance, God's protection—are only approximate. If St. Benedict uses them, it is because of the poverty of human language. In reality (and St. Benedict knows it), God is not a cooperating or helping cause; he is the primary cause and his causality is not added to ours. God is the cause of being in the human order as well as in the process of becoming like him in the supernatural order.

Sole Reliance on God

Humility for St. Benedict does not consist in denying the obvious or ignoring the results of God's work in us. There are, to be sure, two steps in the ladder of humility, the sixth and seventh, that bring home to us our nothingness before God, our essential helplessness, our sinful condition; but at the same time our sense of God's transcendence and perfection is heightened.

"The sixth degree of humility is that a monk be content with the poorest and worst of everything, and that in every occupation assigned him he consider himself a bad and worthless workman, saying with the prophet, 'I am brought to nothing and I am without understanding; I have become as a beast of burden before you, yet I am always with you' (Ps 73:22-23)."

"The seventh degree of humility is that he consider himself lower and of less account than anyone else, and this not only in verbal protestation but also with the most heartfelt inner conviction, humbling himself and saying with the prophet, 'But I am a worm and no man, the scorn of men and the outcast of the people (Ps 22:6).' 'After being exalted, I have been humbled and covered with confusion' (Ps 88:16). And again, 'It is good for me that you have humbled me, that I may learn your commandments' (Ps 119:71)" (R 7). This is the attitude of those disciples who are aware of the deficiencies in their lives and the abuse they make of God's grace.

But St. Benedict also says that the disciple should "praise God's work in him." To do that we must take note of the good in us. But whether we are contemplating our sinfulness or, in happier moments, recognizing the work God is accomplishing in us, we never lose sight of our essential poverty and dependence. In that consists our humility.

We are, by grace, children of God, brothers and sisters of Christ, temples of the Holy Spirit. It is permissible for us to see the good in ourselves and to rejoice over it, like the Virgin Mary: "My soul magnifies the Lord, and my spirit rejoices in God my Savior. . . . All generations will call me blessed" (Luke 1:46-48). The work of God in us remains the property of God. It is good to admire it on the same ground as other works of God. But every good perceived must be referred to its source and author. "You see in me your work and not mine," says St. Augustine; "for, if you took account of my work, you would condemn me; but if you take account of your work, you will reward me. All my good works whatsoever come to me from you. They are more yours than mine."[1]

St. Benedict is a realist; he knows the good and the enemy of the good. The disciple, to say it again, is asked to adopt God's viewpoint and see things as he sees them. Every good tells of God and is the product of his omnipotence. Pride is vain and absurd not because it affirms existent good but because it robs God of what belongs to him. It consists in a distorted vision; instead of seeing the world in its dependence, it makes the creature the center. The axis of the world is shifted.

The more we grow in the practical conviction that when we a left to ourselves nothing happens in the order of salvation, the mo we put our trust in grace and rely on it. From grace we draw th courage, the stout heart that prevents us from considering difficu ties insurmountable. No difficulty, we learn, can withstand God though the route he chooses for overcoming it may not be ours.

In this environment community life can thrive. Divine grace i the milieu, the atmosphere that makes possible the maintenance, the steady growth, and flowering of the supernatural life. From this objective truth established through faith, the soul proceeds to practice Its constant help is not in itself but in the Lord from whom all good flows. Such a course is the opposite of presumption, of trust in oneself where every fall begins.

St. Benedict, then, is not one to put his monastic hope in huma nature. The work of sanctification requires us to begin with humi ity, the conviction and avowal of our radical dependence. We mu cease to stand on our own resources. Given these preliminaries, th essential can be considered accomplished. But God does not retir He called us; he will continue to bestow his daily grace, his untiri care. Every grace carries the seed of further grace. We can be sure the God in whom we place our trust: "Secure in their hope o divine recompense, they go on with joy to declare, 'But in all th trials we conquer, through him who has granted us his love'" (R see Rom 8:37).

---

[1] St. Augustine, *Commentary on Psalm 137*, n. 18, *PL* 37, 1738–1784.

Benedict's words) to which the community gave fervent preparation and "looked forward with the joy of spiritual desire" (R 49). Each week the return of Sunday brought back a portion of the joy of Easter and its Alleluia. Manual work came to a halt; prayer, in one form or another, filled the day: "On Sundays, let all occupy themselves in reading, except those who have been appointed to various duties" (R 48).

Glorification of the Trinity

It is in the Office in particular that St. Benedict demonstrates his Trinitarian faith and devotion. The *Gloria Patri* concludes every psalm and the last responsory of every Nocturn. The psalms were said standing, but since the community sat for the readings and the responsories that followed, St. Benedict prescribes: "As soon as the chanter beings it [*Gloria Patri*], let all rise from their seats in honor and reverence to the Holy Trinity" (R 9).

The *Gloria Patri* was not only a signal for the community to rise; it expressed the saint's deep faith, his love for the three divine Persons. At Monte Cassino it was chanted in its anti-Arian form, with the *Sicut erat* that was commonly added in Italy from before the Council of Vaison in 529. The *Gloria Patri* is added to the Canticles of the Office, to the introductory verse, to the *Suscipe* of the profession ceremony. It recurs over and over in the liturgy of the monastery.

At the night Office on Sundays and feasts St. Benedict introduces a Trinitarian hymn, the *Te Deum*, before the gospel and follows up the reading of the gospel with the *Te decet laus*, a Trinitarian acclamation of praise of Greek origin. Thus two Trinitarian chants frame the gospel and figure in the conclusion to the solemn night Office of Sunday and feast days.

St. Benedict seems to be partial to groupings of three. Does this also come from a desire to honor the Trinity? Among such groupings are the three readings with three responsories in the night Office of ordinary days; the three Nocturns on festive days and the threefold structure of the third Nocturn; the three psalms that form the texture of the small day Hours; the blessing verse for the reader and the kitchen servers repeated three times; the triple *Suscipe* of profession, and so forth.

St. Benedict honors the Trinity and gives special attention to the honor paid to it in the Office. References to the Trinity likewise appear in many passages of the Rule, passages that are among the most important. Even so, the spirituality of the monastery remains centered on Christ, and the spiritual journey to be accomplished under Christ is what preoccupied the Abbot of Monte Cassino. As to the Trinity, he brings the disciple to the threshold of its ineffable mystery and rests with that.

The Work of God

The Work of God is everything the disciple does. This is how the fathers of monasticism understood the term. For St. Benedict, the Work of God is the Divine Office, the chanted community prayer. More personal prayer he calls *oratio* somewhat in the sense that was common in the eighteenth century. As defined by St. Benedict, the Work of God is in some way contracted. It is a work among others in the life of the community, but a work that is absolutely central and to which no other work compares.

St. Benedict is not long in coming to the section of the Rule dealing with the Office. He places it immediately after his ascetical syllabus: the Prologue and the first seven chapters. Having sketched the spiritual profile of his disciple and before taking up the practical organization of the monastery, he sets to work on the structure of the Office and spends a full dozen chapters completing it. Nowhere else he is so precise and so minute.

The disciple is a person of prayer; better still, a pray-er. In monastic circles from the very beginning, the call to unceasing prayer found in the gospel (Luke 18:1) and in St. Paul (1 Thess 5:17) was more than a counsel; it was a rule of life that the community tried to practice. With hermits it took the form of constant thought of God; nightly psalm-praying alternated with silent prayer. By day, at work, psalm-praying continued, though more randomly. Work itself was primarily for some necessary physical activity, but not so as to hinder the activity of the soul.

The cenobitic life brought a new dimension to prayer in the prayer meeting such as the hermits themselves had in the Egyptian desert during the long vigils before Sunday. Given a large group of people gathering for prayer at appointed times, and this every day of their lives, it becomes necessary that some well defined structures govern the proceedings. The Divine Office has not only to reflect each one's effort to achieve continual prayer; it has also to support it and become an introduction, an initiation to constant prayer; in short, a school of the spiritual life.

The community comes together at appointed intervals to help

one another realize a common work; the prayer of one helps the prayer of the other. We are chanters of the divine Majesty. Our Work of God is the dramatization, in community form, of our unceasing converse with God. The Office is ordained to constant prayer; it is its foundation, its irreplaceable base. But the monastic task of prayer goes beyond this reserved and privileged moment when the whole community meets and honors God.

St. Benedict makes a real effort to invest this community gathering with dignity and seriousness of purpose and to make it a true service: "When the Work of God is ended, let all go out in perfect silence, and let reverence for God be observed" (R 52). He does not want long periods of silence during the community prayer that consists almost entirely of formal praise (psalmody) and listening to the word of God along with some chants more lyrical in character, the hymns. For silent prayer he permits greater spontaneity rather than impose a rigid standard on all. Each person can pursue it according to the grace received. The prayer of the Office is regular, pre-arranged, and institutionalized. Benedict makes it a point to dissociate the community praise from the more personal prayer which the disciple may be moved by the Holy Spirit to offer to God during *lectio divina*, or in the privacy of visits to the oratory, or even at daily work now and then broken for moments of prayer.

But the community praise comes first. On this the Abbot of Monte Cassino is inflexible. In the organization of his monastery he assigns a large part to manual labor, and reduces significantly the part which other monastic lawgivers had allotted to psalmody (especially in the monachism of Gaul). But for this very reason he is the more insistent, seeing in this minimum that he demands of all a sacred duty, the summit toward which all monastic activity converges.

As though to impress his point, he commits to the abbot the announcing of the time for the Work of God. Being the head of the community that is formed for the common quest of God, it is he who calls the members to prayer at regular intervals. He holds the place of Christ who came to raise on earth worshipers in spirit and truth: "The indicating of the hour of the Work of God by day and by night shall devolve upon the abbot, either to give the signal himself or to assign this duty to such a careful brother that everything will take place at its proper hours" (R 47). He not only calls the community to prayer but presides. The Lord's Prayer is reserved to him at Lauds and Vespers; he reads the gospel at Matins; he intones the great doxologies; he gives the blessings. It is up to him to see that every-thing at the worshiping assembly proceeds in orderly fashion; it is his duty to choose who will chant or read, and from him latecomers wait to receive the signal to join the community in psalmody.

There are no gray areas in the Divine Office, nothing arbitrary. It is something very definite, something also which the community prepares itself to celebrate worthily, and for which it puts forth every effort to give it the place it must have. The liturgical legisla-tion of St. Benedict is marked by discretion, by consideration of the capacities of his disciples, the flesh-and-blood individuals who form his community and whose limitations he knows.

The Abbot of Monte Cassino respects tradition without exclud-ing the new. He put his own stamp on the structure he found in the Rule of the Master, yet seems more concerned to incorporate the ac-cumulated legacy of past generations. He utilizes books of chant that everyone knew: anthologies of antiphons, responsories and hymns.

St. Benedict's liturgy of the Office is more adoptive than inven-tive; it mirrors, therefore, not only his own community but more generally a community in which his predecessors, simple monks and monastic fathers, could also recognize themselves. Its first debt is to the Bible, from which it borrows what is most prominent: psalms and readings. It also avails itself of inherited musical and poetic treasures and prayer-formulas (orations) originating with the people of God before Benedict. Chanted prayers, modulated readings, lyric pieces alternate without prejudice to the spirit of worshipful recol-lection that St. Benedict has at heart. By the judicious rotation of these diverse elements he keeps his disciples attentive and actively engaged.

Even for the weakest soul Benedict's Office realizes, at least in part, the ideal of continual prayer that attracted numerous genera-tions of monks and ascetics before him. Yet the abbot has also to ex-hort his followers to go further and make all their activities a prayer. *Lectio divina*, properly done, is one of them; it is more individual and private and is guided by the invisible author who wrote what the disciple reads and through the Holy Spirit is still present. But even more is sought. Liturgical prayer will always fall short of its promise unless it inspires authentic contemplation. This is a gift beyond the power of the abbot to hand to his community, but he can and must create the conditions generally necessary for its evolve-ment: e.g., by the teaching he imparts, the reading he recommends, the spirit of silence and recollection he maintains in the community, limitations, our weaknesses, and our unstable and dilatory nature. The author of the Rule wanted to "introduce nothing harsh or burdensome" (R Prol). He weighs the pros and cons; he stretches the measure of indulgence. Yet he is convinced that human limitations can be surmounted through the all-powerful action of grace, and he turns unceasingly to this hidden reserve (too often ignored or slighted) of spiritual energy. He does not commit his disciples to works that have no purpose other than an ascetical exercise, as though an end in itself, but leads them on toward a kind of spiritual self-transcendence; to this he sets no limits, trusting the omnipotence of God to produce marvels of grace.

Grace, then, is absolutely necessary not only to begin a meritorious action but also to sustain it and realize its full potential. Our spiritual effort is a response. God takes the initiative; he speaks, he calls; he touches the heart of the one he calls. We hear the voice inviting us and consent to obey. This obedience is a difficult work; it does not come without effort. We either cooperate with grace or we do not. We possess gifts given by God that we must bring to fruit. God puts at our disposal the instruments to be used. The most valuable of these is the prayer that confesses our helplessness and declares our reliance on God all-powerful. Watchfulness and personal effort are the rule.

Most assuredly, it is with Christ's help and with his grace that any true virtue takes root in the soul. Yet these terms — God's help, God's assistance, God's protection — are only approximate. If St. Benedict uses them, it is because of the poverty of human language. In reality (and St. Benedict knows it), God is not a cooperating or helping cause; he is the primary cause and his causality is not added to ours. God is the cause of being in the human order as well as in the process of becoming like him in the supernatural order.

Sole Reliance on God

Humility for St. Benedict does not consist in denying the obvious or ignoring the results of God's work in us. There are, to be sure, two steps in the ladder of humility, the sixth and seventh, that bring home to us our nothingness before God, our essential helplessness, our sinful condition; but at the same time our sense of God's transcendence and perfection is heightened.

"The sixth degree of humility is that a monk be content with the poorest and worst of everything, and that in every occupation assigned him he consider himself a bad and worthless workman, saying with the prophet, 'I am brought to nothing and I am without understanding; I have become as a beast of burden before you, yet I am always with you' (Ps 73:22-23)."

"The seventh degree of humility is that he consider himself lower and of less account than anyone else, and this not only in verbal protestation but also with the most heartfelt inner conviction, humbling himself and saying with the prophet, 'But I am a worm and no man, the scorn of men and the outcast of the people (Ps 22:6).' 'After being exalted, I have been humbled and covered with confusion' (Ps 88:16). And again, 'It is good for me that you have humbled me, that I may learn your commandments' (Ps 119:71)" (R 7). This is the attitude of those disciples who are aware of the deficiencies in their lives and the abuse they make of God's grace.

But St. Benedict also says that the disciple should "praise God's work in him." To do that we must take note of the good in us. But whether we are contemplating our sinfulness or, in happier moments, recognizing the work God is accomplishing in us, we never lose sight of our essential poverty and dependence. In that consists our humility.

We are, by grace, children of God, brothers and sisters of Christ, temples of the Holy Spirit. It is permissible for us to see the good in ourselves and to rejoice over it, like the Virgin Mary: "My soul magnifies the Lord, and my spirit rejoices in God my Savior. . . . All generations will call me blessed" (Luke 1:46-48). The work of God in us remains the property of God. It is good to admire it on the same ground as other works of God. But every good perceived must be referred to its source and author. "You see in me your work and not mine," says St. Augustine; "for, if you took account of my work, you would condemn me; but if you take account of your work, you will reward me. All my good works whatsoever come to me from you. They are more yours than mine."[1]

St. Benedict is a realist; he knows the good and the enemy of the good. The disciple, to say it again, is asked to adopt God's viewpoint and see things as he sees them. Every good tells of God and is the product of his omnipotence. Pride is vain and absurd not because it affirms existent good but because it robs God of what belongs to him. It consists in a distorted vision; instead of seeing the world in its dependence, it makes the creature the center. The axis of the world is shifted.

---

[1] St. Augustine, *Commentary on Psalm 137*, n. 18, *PL* 37, 1738-1784.

The more we grow in the practical conviction that when we are left to ourselves nothing happens in the order of salvation, the more we put our trust in grace and rely on it. From grace we draw the courage, the stout heart that prevents us from considering difficulties insurmountable. No difficulty, we learn, can withstand God, though the route he chooses for overcoming it may not be ours.

In this environment community life can thrive. Divine grace is the milieu, the atmosphere that makes possible the maintenance, the steady growth, and flowering of the supernatural life. From this objective truth established through faith, the soul proceeds to practice. Its constant help is not in itself but in the Lord from whom all good flows. Such a course is the opposite of presumption, of trust in oneself where every fall begins.

St. Benedict, then, is not one to put his monastic hope in human nature. The work of sanctification requires us to begin with humility, the conviction and avowal of our radical dependence. We must cease to stand on our own resources. Given these preliminaries, the essential can be considered accomplished. But God does not retire. He called us; he will continue to bestow his daily grace, his untiring care. Every grace carries the seed of further grace. We can be sure of the God in whom we place our trust: "Secure in their hope of a divine recompense, they go on with joy to declare, 'But in all these trials we conquer, through him who has granted us his love'" (R 7; see Rom 8:37).

8

Prayer

Benedict's disciples chant much, and the chant is joyous. Love of God, love of Christ account for the monastic life. God's free gift calls for the response of love, freely given like his. The disciple has freely received and freely returns in gladness. It is an inner joy, reflected in song and praise.

Adoration is a duty of the creature. The gospel did not abolish this duty but put it on a higher level by enhancing the relationship that unites creature and Creator. It became a filial relationship marked by freedom and spontaneity.

Religion seeks expression in love and cultic worship inspired by love. The followers of St. Benedict live in community and chant in community. The habitual joy that pervades their life is periodically refreshed in the celebration of Easter, in the celebration of Sunday, the weekly Easter, and the feasts of patron saints. Every celebration was for them a foretaste of the feast of eternity, the eternal Easter: "Love sings now," says St. Augustine, "and love will sing then; but now it is a famished love that sings, then it will be a sated love."[1]

Easter brightens the entire liturgical year, the "holy Easter" (St.

---

[1] St. Augustine, *Sermon 255*, n. 5, *PL* 38, 1183.

Benedict's words) to which the community gave fervent preparation and "looked forward with the joy of spiritual desire" (R 49). Each week the return of Sunday brought back a portion of the joy of Easter and its Alleluia. Manual work came to a halt; prayer, in one form or another, filled the day: "On Sundays, let all occupy themselves in reading, except those who have been appointed to various duties" (R 48).

Glorification of the Trinity

It is in the Office in particular that St. Benedict demonstrates his Trinitarian faith and devotion. The *Gloria Patri* concludes every psalm and the last responsory of every Nocturn. The psalms were said standing, but since the community sat for the readings and the responsories that followed, St. Benedict prescribes: "As soon as the chanter beings it [*Gloria Patri*], let all rise from their seats in honor and reverence to the Holy Trinity" (R 9).

The *Gloria Patri* was not only a signal for the community to rise; it expressed the saint's deep faith, his love for the three divine Persons. At Monte Cassino it was chanted in its anti-Arian form, with the *Sicut erat* that was commonly added in Italy from before the Council of Vaison in 529. The *Gloria Patri* is added to the Canticles of the Office, to the introductory verse, to the *Suscipe* of the profession ceremony. It recurs over and over in the liturgy of the monastery.

At the night Office on Sundays and feasts St. Benedict introduces a Trinitarian hymn, the *Te Deum*, before the gospel and follows up the reading of the gospel with the *Te decet laus*, a Trinitarian acclamation of praise of Greek origin. Thus two Trinitarian chants frame the gospel and figure in the conclusion to the solemn night Office of Sunday and feast days.

St. Benedict seems to be partial to groupings of three. Does this also come from a desire to honor the Trinity? Among such groupings are the three readings with three responsories in the night Office of ordinary days; the three Nocturns on festive days and the threefold structure of the third Nocturn; the three psalms that form the texture of the small day Hours; the blessing verse for the reader and the kitchen servers repeated three times; the triple *Suscipe* of profession, and so forth.

St. Benedict honors the Trinity and gives special attention to the honor paid to it in the Office. References to the Trinity likewise appear in many passages of the Rule, passages that are among the most important. Even so, the spirituality of the monastery remains centered on Christ, and the spiritual journey to be accomplished under Christ is what preoccupied the Abbot of Monte Cassino. As to the Trinity, he brings the disciple to the threshold of its ineffable mystery and rests with that.

The Work of God

The Work of God is everything the disciple does. This is how the fathers of monasticism understood the term. For St. Benedict, the Work of God is the Divine Office, the chanted community prayer. More personal prayer he calls *oratio* somewhat in the sense that was common in the eighteenth century. As defined by St. Benedict, the Work of God is in some way contracted. It is a work among others in the life of the community, but a work that is absolutely central and to which no other work compares.

St. Benedict is not long in coming to the section of the Rule dealing with the Office. He places it immediately after his ascetical syllabus: the Prologue and the first seven chapters. Having sketched the spiritual profile of his disciple and before taking up the practical organization of the monastery, he sets to work on the structure of the Office and spends a full dozen chapters completing it. Nowhere else he is so precise and so minute.

The disciple is a person of prayer; better still, a pray-er. In monastic circles from the very beginning, the call to unceasing prayer found in the gospel (Luke 18:1) and in St. Paul (1 Thess 5:17) was more than a counsel; it was a rule of life that the community tried to practice. With hermits it took the form of constant thought of God; nightly psalm-praying alternated with silent prayer. By day, at work, psalm-praying continued, though more randomly. Work itself was primarily for some necessary physical activity, but not so as to hinder the activity of the soul.

The cenobitic life brought a new dimension to prayer in the prayer meeting such as the hermits themselves had in the Egyptian desert during the long vigils before Sunday. Given a large group of people gathering for prayer at appointed times, and this every day of their lives, it becomes necessary that some well defined structures govern the proceedings. The Divine Office has not only to reflect each one's effort to achieve continual prayer; it has also to support it and become an introduction, an initiation to constant prayer; in short, a school of the spiritual life.

The community comes together at appointed intervals to help

one another realize a common work; the prayer of one helps the prayer of the other. We are chanters of the divine Majesty. Our Work of God is the dramatization, in community form, of our unceasing converse with God. The Office is ordained to constant prayer; it is its foundation, its irreplaceable base. But the monastic task of prayer goes beyond this reserved and privileged moment when the whole community meets and honors God.

St. Benedict makes a real effort to invest this community gathering with dignity and seriousness of purpose and to make it a true service: "When the Work of God is ended, let all go out in perfect silence, and let reverence for God be observed" (R 52). He does not want long periods of silence during the community prayer that consists almost entirely of formal praise (psalmody) and listening to the word of God along with some chants more lyrical in character, the hymns. For silent prayer he permits greater spontaneity rather than impose a rigid standard on all. Each person can pursue it according to the grace received. The prayer of the Office is regular, pre-arranged, and institutionalized. Benedict makes it a point to dissociate the community praise from the more personal prayer which the disciple may be moved by the Holy Spirit to offer to God during *lectio divina*, or in the privacy of visits to the oratory, or even at daily work now and then broken for moments of prayer.

But the community praise comes first. On this the Abbot of Monte Cassino is inflexible. In the organization of his monastery he assigns a large part to manual labor, and reduces significantly the part which other monastic lawgivers had allotted to psalmody (especially in the monachism of Gaul). But for this very reason he is the more insistent, seeing in this minimum that he demands of all a sacred duty, the summit toward which all monastic activity converges.

As though to impress his point, he commits to the abbot the announcing of the time for the Work of God. Being the head of the community that is formed for the common quest of God, it is he who calls the members to prayer at regular intervals. He holds the place of Christ who came to raise on earth worshipers in spirit and truth: "The indicating of the hour of the Work of God by day and by night shall devolve upon the abbot, either to give the signal himself or to assign this duty to such a careful brother that everything will take place at its proper hours" (R 47). He not only calls the community to prayer but presides. The Lord's Prayer is reserved to him at Lauds and Vespers; he reads the gospel at Matins; he intones the great doxologies; he gives the blessings. It is up to him to see that every-thing at the worshiping assembly proceeds in orderly fashion; it is his duty to choose who will chant or read, and from him latecomers wait to receive the signal to join the community in psalmody.

There are no gray areas in the Divine Office, nothing arbitrary. It is something very definite, something also which the community prepares itself to celebrate worthily, and for which it puts forth every effort to give it the place it must have. The liturgical legisla-tion of St. Benedict is marked by discretion, by consideration of the capacities of his disciples, the flesh-and-blood individuals who form his community and whose limitations he knows.

The Abbot of Monte Cassino respects tradition without exclud-ing the new. He put his own stamp on the structure he found in the Rule of the Master, yet seems more concerned to incorporate the ac-cumulated legacy of past generations. He utilizes books of chant that everyone knew: anthologies of antiphons, responsories and hymns.

St. Benedict's liturgy of the Office is more adoptive than inven-tive; it mirrors, therefore, not only his own community but more generally a community in which his predecessors, simple monks and monastic fathers, could also recognize themselves. Its first debt is to the Bible, from which it borrows what is most prominent: psalms and readings. It also avails itself of inherited musical and poetic treasures and prayer-formulas (orations) originating with the people of God before Benedict. Chanted prayers, modulated readings, lyric pieces alternate without prejudice to the spirit of worshipful recol-lection that St. Benedict has at heart. By the judicious rotation of these diverse elements he keeps his disciples attentive and actively engaged.

Even for the weakest soul Benedict's Office realizes, at least in part, the ideal of continual prayer that attracted numerous genera-tions of monks and ascetics before him. Yet the abbot has also to ex-hort his followers to go further and make all their activities a prayer. *Lectio divina*, properly done, is one of them; it is more individual and private and is guided by the invisible author who wrote what the disciple reads and through the Holy Spirit is still present. But even more is sought. Liturgical prayer will always fall short of its promise unless it inspires authentic contemplation. This is a gift beyond the power of the abbot to hand to his community, but he can and must create the conditions generally necessary for its evolve-ment: e.g., by the teaching he imparts, the reading he recommends, the spirit of silence and recollection he maintains in the community, and the elimination of whatever might be an occasion of spiritual dissipation to the disciple.

To Put Nothing Before the Work of God

"At the hour for the Divine Office, as soon as the signal is heard, let them abandon whatever they may have in hand and hasten with the greatest speed, yet with seriousness, so that there is no excuse for levity. Let nothing, therefore, be put before the Work of God" (R 43).

At least twice in the Rule, St. Benedict charges the community to put nothing before the love of Christ. He uses the same expression, "to put nothing before," in reference to the Work of God, as though in his view the Divine Office was the community's most excellent witness to their love of Christ; as though, furthermore, the Divine Office was the preeminent occasion for the practice of this love. Benedict wants the novice to be zealous for the Divine Office. Even for the disciple who is occupied beyond the monastic precincts the Office remains the summit of daily life: "Those brethren who are working at a great distance and cannot get to the oratory at the proper time — the abbot judging that such is the case — shall perform the Work of God where they are working, bending their knees in reverence before God" (R 50). The same applies to those on a journey: "They shall not let the appointed Hours pass by" (*Ibid.*). The Office is, in fact, one of the essential duties of the service that the disciple owes to the Lord who enrolled that person in his army. Making excuses would be out of character, dishonorable; it would be "showing themselves too lazy in the service to which they are vowed" (R 18).

The Office is no better than the spirit one brings to it. Physical presence is not enough. Faith must prevail, faith more alive and perceptive than in any other circumstance: "Let us therefore consider how we ought to conduct ourselves in the sight of the Godhead and of his angels, and let us take part in the psalmody that our mind may be in harmony with our voice" (R 19).

St. Benedict evokes the image of the heavenly Jerusalem and wants to see his community reflect its celestial liturgy. The community is to render its service to the Lord "in fear" and "to sing praise in the sight of the angels" (*Ibid.*). Every function in the oratory is to be performed "with humility, gravity and reverence" (R 47), but above all with care and attention. In the Office the community goes to meet the Lord who is coming; it holds watch for the

One who has announced his return and wants to find his servants vigilant when he comes.

Spontaneous Prayer

There is a definite place for spontaneous prayer in the Office, which provides for moments of silence. But St. Benedict wants it then to be short according to his principle of allowing for individual need or generosity, "that the strong may have something to strive after, and the weak may not fall back in dismay" (R 64).

In some ways private prayer is more difficult and demanding than the common prayer of the Office where the individual is aided by the community and has an assigned place. Some have trouble staying at it, like the restless monk in one of the dozen monasteries of Subiaco: "He would never remain with the rest of the community for silent prayer. Instead he left the chapel as soon as they knelt down to pray, and passed the time aimlessly at whatever happened to interest him" (D 4). This prayer requires even greater recollection than the psalms in choir. St. Gregory speaks of it as "labor."

Benedict prayed much. Gregory shows him frequently at his retreat while the community was at work: he prays, he has a cell apart, not for sleeping (since the Rule wants him to be with the community, see D 35; R 22), but for private prayer and for doing his work. In his cell he had a reed matting for his prostrations. Whenever he felt the need, he ended the conversation, closed the door and immersed himself in prayer; it was a habit of his (D 11). His prayer was attended by tears that normally were not tears of dire distress. He does not cry out but rather weeps softly (but see D 17).

In Chapter 20, On Reverence in Prayer, St. Benedict speaks mostly of the prayer of petition and points out the humility and respect that should accompany it, the purity of heart, and the untainted motivation. Prayer of this kind he wants "short and pure," unless special inspiration of grace prolongs it.

But private prayer is more than petitioning; it is most of all a quest for closer union while awaiting the final consummation: "When the Work of God is ended, let all go out in perfect silence, and let reverence for God be observed, so that any brother who may wish to pray privately will not be hindered by another's misbehavior. And at other times also, if anyone should want to pray by himself, let him go in simply and pray, not in a loud voice but with tears and fervor of heart" (R 52).

St. Benedict wants this prayer to be offered in a quiet and

unobstrusive manner, like the prayer of the publican in the gospel, who also "went in" simply and humbly, not advertising his presence. The disciple in constant search of God is then assured of finding him. The oratory is the favored place to find him. It has no other purpose.

St. Benedict wins our admiration by the balance he achieves between the community life and the individual life of the disciple. He tries to make sure that the collectivity does not encroach upon the more personal prayer and *lectio divina*. Each is permitted to find his or her own measure, according to the grace that person receives.

Praying Always

The disciple's entire life is an effort to pray. This effort is helped along at special times and places designed to revitalize it and make unceasing prayer a reality. To be aware that God is present at all times and at every moment, "in the oratory, in the monastery, in the garden, on the road, in the fields or anywhere else, and whether sitting, walking or standing" (R 7), this in itself is a form of continual prayer. Contact with God is ceaselessly sought, is maintained, is restored when lost. Our presence to God prompts us to see God everywhere, to respond to his omnipresence and to the divine gaze that is ever upon us.

Since human nature is easy prey to distraction and cannot, without special grace, remain attentive over a long time, St. Benedict comes to the aid of the disciple's prayer through such effective means as: public and private reading (*lectio*), memorization of the psalms and recalling them throughout the day, and pauses at work for prayer: "To devote oneself frequently to prayer" (R 4).

There is consequently a great continuity in the life of the disciple, going from the Divine Office to *lectio*, from *lectio* to prayer, from prayer to the refectory, from the refectory to work. Peace accompanies the individual, and silence and the cloister favor one's application to interior prayer. Custody of the heart, mastery of the passions makes for a state of soul in which prayer becomes the air it breathes.

The absence of temporal care because of the disciple's total surrender also facilitates prayer. And the joy that St. Benedict wants to be the habitual mood of his followers (". . . that no one may be troubled or vexed in the house of God," R 31) creates an attitude of thankfulness that is also habitual. Their occupation is to sing God's praise in their hearts and, at specified times, to do so in common, the body reverberating the interior praise. Their whole existence acquires a sacred character. Work, dissociated from the lust of money, becomes unselfish, is anxiety resistant, and generously given.

Like St. Martin, who did not rest from prayer and seemed to be praying even when doing something else, the monk is a staunch pray-er, aspiring to the charismatic gift of unceasing prayer.

Here perhaps is the place to quote a passage from the Rule of the Master that by its insertion in the *Concordia regularis* of Benedict of Aniane no doubt influenced the architecture of monastic buildings: "The monastery should be so well and beautifully designed that wherever one enters, it gives the appearance of a church. Then, wherever the monks assemble, it will be for them a decent, agreeable, and pleasant place to pray" (Rule of the Master, ch. 54, v. 64–65).

The life of the community is therefore dedicated to the praise of God in the comprehensive sense spoken of. The first initiative came from the Lord who by his overtures and call put it under obligation to return thanks. In the Divine Office the community sings formal praise and proclaims the wonderful things God has wrought. It is a glowing testimony, a publicity given to the work of salvation. But it cannot be content with that. From one's lips mounts a continual homage, the expression of one's love. This demands perfect harmony between lips and life. It demands an interior formative principle: total love for the Lord, love undivided and excluding every human action that cannot be reconciled with it.

In this way the disciple's life becomes a unified life. If a person exercises care in the thoughts one entertains, it is to ensure the victory of divine love in one's heart. Praise of God in whatever form, silent or proclaimed, private or public, is a manifestation and fulfillment of this victorious love. Everything in the community — practical organization, ascetical practice, conditions of life, silence, work — is appointed to this one purpose: the glorification of God through continual prayer.

9

human Destiny

St. Benedict's intention was not to set up an idyllic little world, closed upon itself, a sort of ideal commune where all the days would be happy and cares and worries never intruded. His community, despite its stability and fixed location, resembled more the people that Moses led through the wilderness in their journey to the Promised Land.

The Goal

Unbroken joy, lasting happiness are not for this life. From the first pages of the Prologue, St. Benedict tells where he wants to lead his disciples, the destination of the pilgrimage to which he invites them. His vision is eschatological. The goal is to dwell under the tent of the King, to find rest on his holy mountain, above all to see in his kingdom the Lord who has called us.

To stimulate his disciple's desire, St. Benedict unfolds the prospect of arriving at an end which brings union with a beloved Person. There is a call, a journeying, and an arrival. A Person, our love of whom lay dormant, called to us. The heart was quickened, and the body followed. Our whole being embarked upon the journey. What remains is to reach the end of the pilgrimage. Christ, God incarnate, was present at the beginning; he will conduct us along the road, and be there at the end.

St. Benedict also portrays the goal as life and happiness. Every being has an instinct for self-preservation and fulfillment. None can do without it. But the life promised by God has a dimension of the highest and the ultimate; and the happiness he offers is beyond comparison with the happiness we know on earth.

In addition, the Rule speaks of reward and wages. There is no proportion between the work commanded, the work performed, and what God prepares for his workers; it exceeds all expectation. What God rewards in the end are his own gifts, the entrusted talents that the servant made productive under God's watchful care and thanks to his continual help.

The many names given to what awaits the disciple at the end of the journey reflect the inability to describe what in fact is indescribable; it remains hidden as long as the journey lasts, being shrouded in the mystery of God. Until then, it is necessary to go to work, to perform the task undertaken, as the parables of the gospel demonstrate with their picturing of the Christian life as a kind of negotiated employment, a remunerated service. One thing matters: to make it to the end of our journey.

The Possibility of Failure

St. Benedict adheres to gospel teaching. Christ more than once affirmed the fearful possibility of falling short of his love. Monastic life can end in failure, can miss the mark. St. Benedict, a realist, inculcates the fear of hell. He urges his disciples to flee the punishments of hell (R Prol); to beware of stubborn disobedience and rebellion, because the punishment of death will fall on the guilty (R 2); to turn absolutely from ways that seem right to others but end in the depths of hell (R 7); to remain faithful to their profession, knowing that otherwise they will be condemned by him whom they mock (R 58). One does not play games with God.

There is no middle ground, no half success. If the disciple does not make it all the way home, to the end of the journey, that one is forever banished from the face of God. St. Benedict does not let the disciple forget this essential truth. To the ancients, eternal salvation was not an empty word. Bearing in mind all the things God has commanded, one's thoughts should turn frequently to "the hell-fire which will burn for their sins those who despise God, and to the life everlasting which is prepared for those who fear him" (R 7). Two ways are open — the way of life and the way of death, one as real as the other.

For St. Benedict hell is not a fabrication, a scarecrow to keep in line the recalcitrant. He is absolutely convinced of its existence, and confronted with open rebellion, with grave and repeated infractions, he has only one concern: how to rescue the disciple from the brink of destruction, how to save that person's soul. St. Benedict wants the abbot to grieve for this member and spare no effort to retrieve the wayward: "Whatever number of brethren he knows he has under his care, he may be sure beyond doubt that on Judgment Day he will have to give the Lord an account of all these souls" (R 2). If the abbot must use the tool of excommunication, of isolation from the community, its whole purpose is to bring the wrongdoer back to reality, "so that the spirit may be saved in the day of the Lord" (R 25).

The possibility of hell is mentioned a number of times as punishment for those who mishandle the goods of the monastery (R 59), as standing danger for those who foment or participate in dissensions within the monastery or fan the flames of jealousy (R 65).

Fear of hell, however, is only one motive among others, and it does not make the disciple less a person; rather, it serves that person as supplementary guarantee against the weakness of human nature.

It is with this in mind that St. Benedict teaches his followers to anticipate God's judgment upon their actions, to make the same judgment that God would make. He asks this of everyone, more particularly of the abbot: "Let the abbot always bear in mind that at the dread judgment of God there will be an examination. . . ." (R 2). The abbot should do all things in the fear of God, "knowing that beyond a doubt he will have to render an account of all his decisions to God" (R 3). "Let him always think of the account he will have to render to God for all his decisions and his deeds" (R 63). "Let the abbot always bear in mind what a burden he has undertaken and to whom he will have to give an account of his stewardship" (R 64). "But the abbot, for his part, should bear in mind that he will have to render an account to God for all his judgments" (R 65). These instructions apply to all; Benedict does not want irresponsible individuals, perpetual children who act without giving thought to the consequences.

Fear of hell develops the sense of sin; it also teaches the disciples humility, since it makes them realize that in the eyes of God the value of their actions often amounts to nothing. True disciples frequently consider what God thinks of their conduct, and since they are not Pharisees (how could they be, in the presence of God who

sees all!), they find nothing to be proud of. The greater their progress in their quest of God, the more aware they become of their own
helplessness to live worthy of God's regard for them. It overwhelms
them and engulfs them in humility as it does the follower who has
"his head always bowed and his eyes toward the ground. Feeling the
guilt of his sins at every moment, he should consider himself already
present at the dread judgment and constantly say in his heart what
the publican in the gospel said. . . ." (R 7).

There is nothing forlorn in this attitude. The Lord himself pro-
nounced the publican just, because he stood in the truth, his "just"
place. Humble and less trustful of ourselves, we pay more attention
to what God thinks of us. We discover or rediscover our vulnerabil-
ity to things that do not square with the Lord who chose us, and we
rely the more on God. We also become most vigilant, watching our
hearts in particular, the only hearts over which we have direct con-
trol. Only there, within ourselves, do we have the certainty of being
able to increase the Kingdom of God. No duty relieves us from the
duty to promote God's growth in ourselves.

A final word. Fear of hell must not be carried to the point that
it cripples activity or becomes an obsession. With this proviso, it has
its place among motives of conduct if only because our neglect of
hell does not suppress its existence.

The Thought of Death

If it is right to fear hell, to experience a certain dread of the
abyss into which we could fall, the reason is that God's judgment
should inspire fear; not fright but fear, i.e., respect, or a kind of
half-worried expectation together with hope in the outcome and
humility before the Judge.

The day of judgment is certainly coming. At the end of life we
will come face to face with the Lord whom we sought, well, poorly,
or moderately well. "Let us live as pilgrims," says St. Augustine; "let
us remember that we are passing through, and we shall sin less;
above all, let us give thanks to the Lord our God because it was his
will that the last day of our life should neither be postponed, nor be
certain."[1] But that the day is coming is certain, and the certainty
keeps us on course. We learn to live in the light, and away from the
shadows, faithful to our profession and shunning the temptation to
compromise.

---

[1] St. Augustine, *Sermon 301*, n. 9, *PL* 38, 1385.

The thought of death accompanies us, but it is not a depressing thought; rather the contrary. We are pilgrims to the mountain of the Lord. Pilgrims do not dread the moment of arrival at their destination; neither are we overcome with anxiety. There will be a change, not in God who is ever the same, but in us; our separated souls will experience being in the presence of the Lord who appraises all things at their true value.

"To keep death daily before one's eyes" (R 4). The disciple remembers to do this. Death has always been the great preoccupation of people, the major problem treated in literature. Thinkers of the world have tried to make sense out of life, so rich and beautiful yet marred by pain and sorrow and seemingly ending in destruction. The disciple knows neither their gnawing anxieties nor their doubts, refuses to settle down in the world as though never to leave it, but adopts instead the attitude of the friends of God: the prophet Simeon ("Lord, now lettest thou they servant depart in peace," Luke 2:29), the apostle Paul ("My desire is to depart and be with Christ," Phil 1:23). We keep the decisive moment before our eyes as an incentive to live according to God and achieve the detachments of our profession. Thanks to the thought of death, we disencumber and simplify our existence. Our whole life becomes a preparation.

Return to God

Monastic life is defined as a conversion or return by way of obedience, a way to salvation. Comparisons are many: it is a search, quest, response; a race and a journey; warfare and combat. *Conversio* evolves into *conversatio*, a way of life, a pattern of behavior, moral conduct.

The disciple leaves the land of disobedience, of neglect and rebellion toward God, and goes in search of the heavenly Jerusalem: one's whole life is directed to this goal. A call brought a turnaround. We abandoned the way we had been going and pointed our lives toward their true end. We do not tread aimlessly, like the vagabond monks of the first chapter; we concentrate on the high road despite the difficulties of the first steps. When, as it will, the pain of conversion sets in, "do not be at once dismayed and fly from the way of salvation, whose entrance cannot but be narrow" (R Prol). St. Benedict assures the newcomer that this is a phase, a stage in one's evolution as a disciple; it will pass. That we may step along more freely, we wrap our raiment around us and set out for the prize, clearing our path of obstacles and doing battle along the way, like Perceval in arduous quest of the Grail.

Monastic life is not an easy road to follow, a life of ease, even though some charge it with being an escape. It requires struggle against Satan and against faults. In the cenobitic community the novice is trained in combat under seasoned soldiers who lend the newcomer support and muster up the novice's courage. The weapons are the gospel, the instruments of good works, and most of all obedience. Several times St. Benedict cautions the novice not to give occasion to "the evil one," hence to be on guard, to look to the right and to the left, to concentrate one's forces where the enemy is strongest.

The disciple battles and does not parley. As soon as the adversary is revealed, we look to our defenses and have recourse to Christ: "When evil thoughts come into one's heart, to dash them against Christ immediately" (R 4). "Under any temptation from the malicious devil, he has brought him to naught by casting him and his temptation from the sight of his heart, and has laid hold of his thoughts while they are still young and dashed them against Christ" (R Prol).

"Are you struggling with a great enemy?" St. Benedict read in St. Augustine's Commentary on the Psalms: "Destroy him on the rock. Is it a lesser adversary? Dash him on the rock. And the great, destroy them on the rock. And the small, dash them on the rock. Let the rock overcome."[2]

St. Benedict also speaks of a climb, of degrees, of a ladder; the goal is to reach a summit. But he is most given to the idea of running. Walking, climbing is not enough; one must make haste and run, run *straight ahead*, not waste time on detours. A characteristic touch: In the Prologue, Benedict quotes the Gospel of St. John: "Walk while you have the light" (12:35). His rendition is, "*Run* while you have the light."

Despite the unhurried demeanor, the prudent reserve, Benedict is a man driven. He wants all things done promptly and with a will. Obedience is immediate: at the call from sleep, one is quickly on one's feet; when the poor knock at the gate, see them at once; when the bell rings for the Divine Office, the word is alacrity. No delay, no hesitation, but joyous zeal, the acceleration of the heart: in short, running toward the Lord. The picture of the ideal disciple precisely is one of a person pointed straight ahead toward an invisible goal; such a one does not dwell on obstacles, being confident that God

---

[2] St. Augustine, *Commentary on Psalm 136*, n. 22, PL 37, 1174.

will provide — a person impelled and inspired by an ardent desire.

Desire for God

In a real sense, we do live in this world. But we thirst for something else. We are cheered and propelled by an overriding hope. Externally, we give the impression of quiet reserve; inwardly, we are running toward the heavenly Jerusalem, to hurl ourselves into the arms of God.

St. Augustine writes: "O the good things of my God that are so delightful! Things imperishable, incomparable, things eternal, unchanging. When shall I see you, O good things of my God? I believe that I shall see you, but not on this earth where death obtains. I believe that I shall see the good things of the Lord in the land of the living. He will deliver me from this earth where death obtains, the God who for love of me deigned to come into the world of mortals and die by the hand of mortals."[3]

The intensity of desire increases as the disciple approaches the goal, since the taste for God grows in proportion as the Lord gives himself. "To desire eternal life with all the passion of the spirit," declares St. Benedict in the Rule (4). The love of Christ is an unceasing cry for his manifestation, for his return.

"Whoever you are, therefore, who are hastening to the heavenly homeland . . ." (R 73). Unlike some monastic authors, St. Benedict does not tell his followers to treat the world with contempt; he only directs them "to become a stranger to the world's ways" (R 4). We allow worldly things their place, but that is a subordinate one; we accept their function as pure means. But we are not taken by them because our love is somewhere else. We rise above them, knowing that we have been richly endowed with a life that is divine. The promise of this eternal life, ever present in our minds, dulls the attraction of the world of sense.

Desire for God becomes more eager, more pure according as the disciple matures. Motivation is more perfect and on a higher plane. The soul expands but the world cannot contain it. This is the joyous state spoken of both at the end of the Prologue and at the end of the chapter on humility. The soul remembers the zeal that the God of the Bible has shown in its regard (the zeal of love imperious and jealous, exclusive and victorious), and in turn is consumed with

---

[3] *Idem, Commentary on Psalm 26*, n. 22, PL 36, 210.

the good zeal that "separates from vices and leads to God and to life everlasting" (R 72). St. Benedict urges his followers to practice this zeal "with the most fervent love" (*Ibid.*), and gives suggestions how to do it. The life of virtue, the life of prayer, the whole monastic observance then breathes an air of fervent charity that gives life priceless value. If there is on earth a foretaste of eternal blessedness, it is found in the one who runs with expanded heart, "with unspeakable sweetness of love" (R Prol), and has rid the soul of its obstacles to the Lord's Kingdom.

10

all together

In St. Gregory's account, Benedict the boy appears rather less than sociable or gregarious. Though a likable youth, he seems to prefer not to mingle with his peers, feeling a need to be alone. His vocation was the hermit's, and when, twice in his life, he turned from the solitary course, each time it was only after considerable persuasion. The second time, in fact, the community had more or less to impose itself on him. Disciples naturally grouped around this master of the spiritual life, as often happened in monastic history.

But it was God, through circumstances and events, who devised the cenobitic vocation of the Abbot of Monte Cassino. The Rule shows to what extent the vocation succeeded; toward the end, in conclusion of the second last chapter, Benedict writes these words: "Let [the brethren] prefer nothing whatever to Christ. And may he brings us *all together* to life everlasting!" (R 72) The metamorphosis was complete, the hermit is now the confirmed cenobite, his only consideration the common life whose spiritual benefits had grown on him as his experience in dealing with souls ripened.

The cenobitic community is the setting in which the disciple's whole life unfolds, and in which one's contemplative prayer aspires to and is fulfilled in "the loftier heights of doctrine and virtue"

(R 73). In the Prologue, Benedict had in effect written, "Never departing from his school, but persevering *in the monastery* according to his teaching until death, we may by patience share in the sufferings of Christ and deserve to have a share also in his kingdom" (R Prol). Though he still admits the superiority of hermits, if not of the eremitical life as such, they no longer claim his attention. He gives them their due in the first chapter, and that is the last we hear of them. Their vocation seemed too individualistic to be taken into account in the Rule he was writing: "Passing these over, therefore [hermits, vagabond monks, monks without a superior], let us proceed, with God's help, to lay down a rule for the strongest kind of monks, the cenobites" (R 1).

In St. Benedict we do not find the rather romantic attraction to the common life that St. Augustine experienced: "How good it is, how sweet, to dwell together as brothers. These words of the psalm, this chant full of sweetness, this ravishing melody which one finds not only in the song but also in the meaning itself, has given birth to entire monasteries. This is the chant that has inspired brethren to dwell together; this verse has been a clarion call to them; it has resounded in the whole world, and those who were divided, were reunited."[1]

St. Benedict's perception is more realistic, more dispassionate and objective, so to speak. It was in his monastic maturity that he came to realize as never before the irreplaceable value of the common life.

The Monastery-Church

In the Rule of the Master, St. Benedict had read of the monastery as a family. His own community was like that, with a father, with sons, with every age of life represented there, from the oldest to the child-oblate. But Benedict is careful not to overdo this aspect, and even corrects the Master on it. He did not want to be misunderstood, did not want anyone to think of his monastery as a kind of transplanted human family with its retinue of doting relatives. To him the reality was more profound, and his ideal also is more demanding.

The military terminology he uses should likewise be viewed in perspective. It did not mean that his monastery was a barracks. Definitely not. More to the mark are several implicit quotations from St. Cyprian that describe the Church as an army in battle

---

[1] St. Augustine, *Commentary on Psalm 132*, n. 7, PL 37, 1729.

array, whose ranks are occupied by soldiers of Christ, one support-
ing the other, all the product of a common training and instruction.
This was the discipline that made the Christian martyr. This also is
the monastery, like the Church in combat against the devil and the
forces of evil. The disciple is prepared for combat after the manner
that Christians during the persecutions were readied for martyr-
dom. St. Benedict often speaks of his monastery as a Church, the
"house of God." No one in it should be grieved (R 31). But it calls for
prudent management by prudent men (R 53). In the person of the
abbot it receives a faithful steward (R 64).

In the two chapters treating of things necessary for the community, St. Benedict refers to chapter four of the Acts of the Apostles; this describes the apostolic community of Jerusalem as it existed
shortly after Pentecost, a gathering where communal sharing was
practiced (R 33, 34). When writing his Rule he had before him this
model that throughout the history of the Church had such a great influence on various movements identified as "apostolic." The
monastery, accordingly, has the Church as its model; more particularly, the primitive Church. What St. Cyprian had said of the
bishop, St. Benedict repeats for the abbot. On the other hand, St.
Gregory the Great frequently applies to the Bishop of Rome, the
universal Shepherd, what St. Benedict had written of the abbot.

In the Rule, as a matter of fact, pastoral terminology is used
constantly: shepherd, sheep, sheepfold, flock. Terms traditionally
employed to describe the role and functions of the bishop are trans-
posed to the monastic plane, with the result that the monastery
assumes the aspect of a Church in miniature. This is not developed
by St. Benedict in any formal way, and there is no central passage or
section in the Rule to which one might point. But there are scattered
references which, taken together, warrant the conclusion that this
was in fact St. Benedict's thought: marginal notations, so to speak,
pointing to a doctrine essentially present but from which he declines
to draw every last ramification.

And with good reason because the monastery, though con-
ceived on the model of a Church, strictly speaking is not a Church.
Its shepherd is not of the hierarchical line founded on the sacrament
of orders and instituted by Christ. The priest received into the community, not without some hesitation, knows from the first moment
that he is not to intervene simply as priest in the government of the
monastery: "Let him not presume to do anything [i.e., on his own],
knowing that he is subject to the discipline of the Rule; but rather let

him give an example of humility to all. If there happens to be question of an appointment or of some business in the monastery, let him expect the rank due him according to the date of his entrance into the monastery, and not the place granted him out of reverence for the priesthood" (R 60). Furthermore, "Let him always keep the place which he received on entering the monastery, except in his duties at the altar or in case the choice of the community and the will of the abbot should promote him for the worthiness of his life" (R 62).

The structure of the monastery parallels the structure of the local Church of Christ, but the hierarchy that governs the monastery is independent of the place held by members of the monastery in the hierarchy of the priesthood. The monastery is not, in this respect, a particular or local Church. It only aims to exemplify, in a manner visible to the whole Church, the ideal of holiness for which the Church exists and also to attract all souls to the Jerusalem above, the Church of heaven.

The Community

St. Benedict, with full forethought, made a choice of the common life. The disciple enrolls in a school, a workshop, an army, a combat force. Such a one is integrated into a group; there is no isolation. The monastery, however, is not necessarily a homogeneous community; strong individual differences can and usually do show up. In what perhaps was more than a witticism, St. Bernard suggests that the communities governed by the Rule house four kinds of monks, including the three that St. Benedict had excluded. There are the unstable individuals (the vagabonds), the quarrelsome and troublemakers (those without a superior), the loners (hermits), and the true cenobites.

Benedict saw tremendous advantages in this insertion of the members into an environment created for the express purpose of a common effort toward a common ideal. First and most important, through the community the individual receives the necessary formation and learns how to combat the devil. Careful direction is always at hand. There is encouragement to go forward, to make new progress. A disciple is brought in line when he or she strays, is corrected and disciplined if need be. The communal society is a powerful help to every follower in seeking God. This why the person comes to the monastery, not just to be with agreeable companions but to seek God, to form and reform one's life. The community contributes mightily to this monastic education of each of its members.

St. Augustine had put much stress on the oneness of mind and heart and the sharing of resources in the monastery. For him, this was the essential. Of humility, obedience, silence and the Divine Office he speaks hardly at all. He was much more interested in the fact of the common life than in its practical organization. The whole monastic ideal consisted in mutual charity and the accommodation of differences of temperament, habit, and education. The common life, in short, impressed St. Augustine as the best way to fulfill the commandment of love of neighbor. St. Benedict was attracted by this ideal and retained its essential ingredients. But his dream for the common life is more complex. He sees in the monastic community the means of practicing more perfectly another form of the commandment of love: obedience.

Obedience, he says, is given to God (R 5). Is it because the abbot who gives the command is the infallible interpreter of God's mind? The abbot, to be sure, has always to avail himself of every possible guarantee of the divine will and as far as humanly possible make sure that he is not prescribing anything that is "against the Lord's precepts" (R 2). But St. Benedict does not claim for him the charismatic gift of infallibility even when he applies to him St. Luke's words: "He who hears you, hears me" (Luke 10:16; R 5). Besides, a request or command can come from many quarters: officials of the monastery, even rank and file members: Let them "vie in paying obedience one to another," writes St. Benedict in Chapter 72.

In accepting and agreeing to follow orders coming from a fellow mortal, the disciples learn to free themselves from themselves; they learn to curb their own wills so as to be completely at the call of God's will: "Not living according to their own choice nor obeying their own desires and pleasures but walking by another's judgment and command, they dwell in monasteries and desire to have an abbot over them" (R 5).

In the beginning of monastic life, obedience has an educative value. The novices, unlearned in the art of seeking God, are placed under the direction of a more experienced senior. They trust their master and bend their own judgment, still spiritually immature, to the judgment of their mentor. Obedience practiced in a community, which is the obedience St. Benedict writes about, has another purpose: to ensure the common good of the group. It is up to the abbot to unify the efforts of all and procure the proper functioning of the community. Even when an order seems untimely or open to question, the disciple agrees to carry out the will of the one charged with promoting the good of the group. Furthermore, because of the precautions the abbot takes to ensure that his orders reflect the divine will, obedience, in the third place, gives the disciples every confidence that they are doing what God intends. The positive commands of the abbot spell out the rules by which they arrive at their goal; without real obedience to these norms made explicit by the abbot, it is not possible to attain the end—anymore than the runner reaches the mark if he stops running.

But obedience according to St. Benedict goes still further; it assures the total liberty of love by the surrender of the good most properly our own: our personal wills. Through a life of obedience in the community, the disciple is weaned from every passing good, as well as schooled in its mortality. Obedience is a means of perfection, a means of deliverance from the self in order that love may be unimpeded. From this point of view obedience, far from being an abdication of the will, is its affirmation; for it relieves the fears and constraints normally experienced by the subject. A person loses his or her life to find it, and one loses one's freedom only to regain it. Obedience establishes the soul of the disciple in liberty.

Relations within the Community

In St. Benedict's design, the abbot is the cornerstone of the community. Like Christ, whose place he holds, he is teacher, shepherd, spiritual guide, physician. He maintains and interprets the law. He is the arbiter who decides how the community is to be governed. His charismatic grace, or grace of state, puts him in the category of the commissioned teachers, the *didascaloi*[2] of the primitive Church. Like the desert fathers, he exerts spiritual fatherhood. But his office embraces every phase of the monastery, and he has the right to share it with others in the community: the deans, the master of novices, the cellarer for overseeing the temporalities.

His task is heavy because his responsibility extends to every domain, without exception: "The abbot should always remember what he is and what he is called, and should know that to whom more is committed, from him more is required. Let him understand also what a difficult and arduous task he has undertaken: ruling souls and adapting himself to a variety of characters" (R 2).

Essentially, his task is twofold. He must govern his community, the house of God, organizing it in such a way that each one may find

---

[2] Teachers entrusted with presenting the Christian message in the primitive Church.

the right environment for the search for God. And secondly, he must provide sound spiritual direction for his community.

The powers given the abbot by St. Benedict are very generous, but he also keeps him mindful of his responsibilities and requires him to use his powers in a fatherly manner. He is not lord and master in the human or pejorative sense; he is a man "for others," who gives of himself and thinks only of being profitable to his followers: "He must be learned in the divine law, that he may have a treasure of knowledge from which to bring forth new things and old. He must be chaste, sober, and merciful. Let him exalt mercy above judgment, so that he himself may obtain mercy. He should hate vices; he should love the brethren" (R 64).

St. Benedict wants for abbot a man who is wise, prudent, and self-mastered, a man of character, dedicated, even-tempered and with a certain gravity about him; but most of all he wants him to be a man of heart, a monk with a passion for souls who spares himself no effort and no pain to win them for God. It can be said that the well-being of the monastery hangs entirely by the paternal grace of the abbot.

Men of this caliber, however, and of such marked personality will not be found in the community unless the prevailing climate favors the development of their human and monastic qualities. The abbot should see to it that this climate exists. The helpers given him by St. Benedict are not perpetual minors. The cellarer is described as "one chosen from the community who is wise, of mature character, sober, not a great eater, not haughty, not excitable, not offensive, not slow, not wasteful, but a God-fearing man who may be like a father to the whole community" (R 31). The master of novices shall be "a senior who is skilled in winning souls" (R 58); the deans, "brethren of good repute and holy life," capable of "taking charge of their deaneries in all things," men with whom "the abbot may with confidence share his burdens" (R 21). The guest master shall be "a brother whose soul is possessed by the fear of God"; for care must be taken that "the house of God be managed by prudent men in a prudent manner" (R 53). For porter, let the abbot choose "a wise old man, who knows how to receive and to give a message" (R 66).

St. Benedict had misgivings about the office of Prior in which he could see more drawbacks than advantages. But if need be, let one be chosen, though the qualifications he lays down are even more numerous than for others (R 65).

It is understood that the abbot's helpers must follow his directions and answer to him for the performance of their office. All, however, are men of government, themselves charged with grave responsibilities.

In St. Augustine, St. Benedict found a monasticism based largely on brotherly love and human joy. The Rule of the Master, on the other hand, tended to favor abbatial authority and its importance in community life. St. Benedict himself, authority conscious though he was, nevertheless is more like St. Augustine in displaying a sensitivity to individual needs and the relationships that bind member to member. This is especially true in the later chapters. There one finds a pattern of thought that in many ways retraces chapters dealing with basic monastic virtues at the beginning of the Rule. That he ends as he begins, articulating cenobitic virtue, is itself a testimonial to the value he places on community life.

The stability that binds the disciple perpetually to the community gives monastic relations a depth and permanence not otherwise possible. All share in the joys and sorrows of each, and each receives from all. Community love is the law that governs the conventual life as well as warms and inspires it.

St. Benedict's disciples honor and respect each other. The aura is not one of camaraderie, as it were, but of deep affection, familial and not familiar. The juniors obey the older members "with all charity and solicitude" (R 71), and honor them, while the older ones show affection to the younger (R 63). But it is chapter 72 especially that deserves to be quoted at length:

"Thus they should anticipate one another in honor [St. Benedict had already said as much in Chapter 63]; most patiently endure one another's infirmities, whether of body or of character; vie in paying obedience one to another — no one following what he considers useful for himself, but rather what benefits another —; tender the charity of brotherhood chastely; fear God in love; love their abbot with a sincere and humble charity; prefer nothing whatever to Christ. And may he bring us all together to life everlasting."

This is the price for the community to become a sign of God to the world, and to its members the means of going to God. The monastery built on the model of the primitive Church is both a foreshadowing and a foretaste of the heavenly Jerusalem, the Church in glory, toward which all its members are moving under the leadership of the abbot.

Conclusion

No one becomes a master without being a disciple. St. Benedict is an excellent example. Before becoming teacher to generations to come, he had pondered and benefited from a legacy of the past. He sifted it and made much of it his own. Only then did he presume to put his charismatic gift to use and improve upon the tradition he had received. Because he had been a disciple in the full force of the word, the future, fifteen hundred years of Western monasticism, belonged to him. What he had received from his monastic forebears provided the incentive for his own efforts. And since God had given him a special grace of spiritual discernment, it was through him that his followers became beneficiaries of the past and retained a bond with earlier centuries of monasticism.

According to St. Augustine, the highest form of charity is the giving of doctrine. No good can compare with the gift of God's light, the light of life. In giving his Rule to the Western world, St. Benedict of Nursia bequeathed a masterpiece, the fruit of his love for his followers as well as proof and testimony of his own charity. In large measure, the spirituality of the West derives from this source and has constantly been nourished by it. The spiritual fatherhood and the charity of Benedict have therefore extended not to thousands or hundreds of thousands but to millions of souls.

From the moment of its appearance in history, the Rule made its influence felt. And this influence has never ceased. At first it shared acceptance with other rules, mostly St. Columban's. But beginning with the Carolingian period, it more or less preempted the field and gained recognition as the one pattern of monastic life.

This is not to say that interpreters of the Rule never disagreed. Controversies did arise between different families of followers claiming the authority of St. Benedict, but it is significant that these disagreements bore on extrinsic and accidental observances and never touched the essentials of his message. Rather than creating divisions, the Rule actually was an agent of deep unity. It may not have the answer to every problem that arises with the founding of a community at a given time or in a given culture; but it is always there to recall to every generation what is essential to monastic life, the bone and marrow without which this life would not be what it is. Thanks to the Rule, monks of all time have shared in the vision of faith of their spiritual father, Benedict of Nursia.

Select Bibliography

Clarkson, Benedict. "The Rule of Saint Benedict and the Concept of Self-Actualization." *Cistercian Studies*, 10 (1975), 22–45.

Deseille, Placide. "Eastern Christian Sources of the Rule of Saint Benedict." *Monastic Studies*, 11 (1975), 73–122.

Gregory the Great, Pope St. *Life and Miracles of St. Benedict (Book Two of the Dialogues)*. Trans. Odo J. Zimmermann, O.S.B., and Benedict R. Avery, O.S.B. Collegeville, Minnesota: The Liturgical Press, 1949.

Leclercq, Jean, O.S.B. "Profession According to the Rule of Saint Benedict." *Rule and Life. An Interdisciplinary Symposium.* Ed. M. Basil Pennington, O.C.S.O. Cistercian Studies Series: Number 12. Spencer, Mass.: Cistercian Publications, 1971, 117–149.

McCann, Justin. *Saint Benedict: The Story of the Man and his Work.* Garden City, N.Y.: Doubleday, 1958 (revised edition).

Mitchell, Nathan, O.S.B. "Ordo Psallendi in the Rule: Historical Perspectives." *American Benedictine Review*, 20 (1969), 505–527.

Peifer, Claude J., O.S.B. *Monastic Spirituality.* New York: Sheed and Ward, 1966.

Raabe, Augusta, O.S.B. "Discernment of Spirits in the Prologue to the Rule of Saint Benedict." *American Benedictine Review*, 23 (1972), 397–423.

Rees, Daniel and Others. *Consider Your Call*. London: SPCK, 1978.
Rippinger, Joel, O.S.B. "The Biblical and Monastic Roots of Poverty in the *Rule* of Benedict under the Aspect of Koinonia." *American Benedictine Review*, 27 (1976), 321–331.
Roberts, Augustine. "Spiritual Methods in Benedictine Life, Yesterday and Today." *Cistercian Studies*, 10 (1975), 207–233.
Rule of Benedict, 1980. Ed. Timothy Fry, O.S.B., and Others. Collegeville, Minnesota: The Liturgical Press, 1980.
Rule of Benedict, The. Ed. and trans. Justin McCann. Westminster, Md.: The Newman Press, 1952.
St. Benedict's Rule for Monasteries. Trans. Leonard J. Doyle. Collegeville, Minnesota: The Liturgical Press, 1948.
Seasoltz, R. Kevin, O.S.B. "Monastic Hospitality." *American Benedictine Review*, 25 (1974), 427–459.
Steidle, Basilius, O.S.B. *The Rule of Saint Benedict*. Trans. Urban J. Schnitzhofer, O.S.B. Canon City, Colorado: Holy Cross Abbey, 1967.
Van der Wielen, Adalbert, O.S.B. "A Method of Prayer according to the Rule of Saint Benedict." *Cistercian Studies*, 11 (1976), 137–149.
Van Zeller, Hubert, O.S.B. *The Holy Rule. Notes on Saint Benedict's Legislation for Monks*. New York: Sheed and Ward, 1958.
Vogüé, Adalbert de, O.S.B. *The Community and Abbot in the Rule of Saint Benedict*. Trans. Charles Philippi. Cistercian Studies Series: 5/1, Kalamazoo, Mich.: Cistercian Publications, 1979.
_____. *"Prayer in the Rule of Saint Benedict." Monastic Studies*, 7 (1969), 113–140.
_____. *"Sub Regula vel Abbate:* The Theological Significance of the Ancient Monastic Rules." *Rule and Life. An Interdisciplinary Symposium*. Ed. M. Basil Pennington, O.C.S.O. Cistercian Studies Series: Number 12. Spencer, Mass.: Cistercian Publications, 1971, 21–63.
Wathen, Ambrose, O.S.B. "The Exegencies of Benedict's Little Rule for Beginners: RB 72." *American Benedictine Review*, 29 (1978), 41–66.
_____. "Relevance of the Rule Today." *American Benedictine Review*, 19 (1968), 234–253.

+ J.T.

*To understand and celebrate
the spirit of St. Benedict:*

LIFE AND MIRACLES OF ST. BENEDICT. By Pope St. Gregory the Great. Translated by Fathers Odo Zimmermann, O.S.B., and Benedict Avery, O.S.B. This is the only historical source we have for the life and character of St. Benedict, written by the monk-Pope Gregory. 96 pages, softbound, $.75.

❖

ST. BENEDICT'S RULE FOR MONASTERIES. Translated by Leonard J. Doyle, Obl.S.B., from the third edition of the Latin text as edited by Dom Cuthbert Butler of Downside Abbey in England. 106 pages, softbound, $1.00.

❖

NOVENA TO ST. BENEDICT. This nine-day prayer, suitable for public or private celebration, honors St. Benedict under the titles of saint, monk, father, lawgiver, miracle worker, prophet, teacher, apostle, and man of God. 40 pages, softbound, $.75.

❖

A BENEDICTINE BOOK OF SONG. By Benedictine composers to commemorate the 1500th anniversary of the birth of St. Benedict in 1980. This songbook features over sixty hymns for seasons, feasts, and rites of the Church, and Eucharistic service music for both monastic and parish congregations. Choir/accompaniment edition, $9.95. Congregation edition, $1.95.

❖

WORSHIP AND WORK. By Father Colman Barry, O.S.B. This is a reprint of the popular centennial history of St. John's Abbey first published in 1956 and now updated with the addition of a 70-page epilog and 10 pages of new photographs. The struggles of the pioneer Benedictines evolves into the ongoing efforts of the St. John's community to give practical expression of the renewal of religious life called for by Vatican II. 424 pages, softbound, $12.50.